King Charles III

Will Happen To The World In His Reign

(The King Of The United Kingdom And 14 Other Commonwealth Realms)

Gerard Thomas

Published By **Simon Dough**

Gerard Thomas

All Rights Reserved

King Charles III: Will Happen To The World In His Reign (The King Of The United Kingdom And 14 Other Commonwealth Realms)

ISBN 978-1-77485-890-5

No part of this guidebook shall be reproduced in any form without permission in writing from the publisher except in the case of brief quotations embodied in critical articles or reviews.

Legal & Disclaimer

The information contained in this ebook is not designed to replace or take the place of any form of medicine or professional medical advice. The information in this ebook has been provided for educational & entertainment purposes only.

The information contained in this book has been compiled from sources deemed reliable, and it is accurate to the best of the Author's knowledge; however, the Author cannot guarantee its accuracy and validity and cannot be held liable for any errors or omissions. Changes are periodically made to this book. You must consult your doctor or get professional medical advice before using any of the suggested remedies, techniques, or information in this book.

Upon using the information contained in this book, you agree to hold harmless the Author from and against any damages, costs, and expenses, including any legal fees potentially resulting from the application of any of the information provided by this guide. This disclaimer applies to any damages or injury caused by the use and application, whether directly or indirectly, of any advice or information presented, whether for breach of contract, tort, negligence, personal injury, criminal intent, or under any other cause of action.

You agree to accept all risks of using the information presented inside this book. You need to consult a professional medical practitioner in order to ensure you are both able and healthy enough to participate in this program.

TABLE OF CONTENTS

Introduction 1

Chapter 1: The Early Years, Education And Family 4

Chapter 2: "A King Waiting To Be King" .. 35

Chapter 3: A Modern (Ish) Young Man ... 55

Chapter 4: Controversy 76

Chapter 5: Family Matters 87

Chapter 6: Diana 106

Chapter 7: Awareness Of The Natural Environment 137

Chapter 8: Philosophy And Religion. Concerns 153

Conclusion 183

Introduction

Charles Philip Arthur George, King of the United Kingdom, and 14 other Commonwealth kingdoms were born on the 14th of November 1948. Following the demise of Elizabeth II, he was elevated into the royal throne on Sept. 8th 2022. He was 73 years old. most long-serving successor apparent of British history, and also the longest-serving person to be crowned king.

Prince Charles was the only grandchild of King George VI and Queen Elizabeth and was the first child of Princess Elizabeth the Duchess of Edinburgh and Philip Duke of Edinburgh. He attended similar Cheam as well as Gordonstoun schools as his father attended. Then, he attended for a full year in The Timbertop campus at Geelong Grammar School in Victoria, Australia. After receiving a BA degree at Cambridge, Charles spent 1971-1976 working as a member of the Royal Air Force and Royal

Navy. He was married in 1981. got married to Diana Spencer. Diana Spencer, and their union was blessed by twins Prince William as well as Prince Harry. The couple separated in 1996 after the reports of their affairs was widely reported. After a fatal car accident in Paris in the year following, Diana lost her life. After 2005, Charles was married for the second time to long-time girlfriend, Camilla Parker Bowles.

As the Prince of Wales, Charles performed formal obligations on behalf of Elizabeth II. He founded the Prince's Trust for young people in 1976. He also sponsors his own charity, the Prince's Charities, and is a patron, president or member of more than 400 other charities and associations. He has advocated for the preservation of older structures and has emphasized the importance of architecture within society. Charles, a modernist architectural critic was involved in the development of Poundbury which is an innovative town that was inspired by his architectural style. He is also the editor and author or co-author on several books.

As the renowned manager in charge of Charles was the renowned manager of Duchy of Cornwall estates, Charles was an environmentalist who fought for organic agriculture and climate change actions that earned him prizes and recognition from environmental organizations. Charles is also a voice against genetically engineered food. Charles his support for homeopathy as well as other alternative treatments has been criticized. The conduct at one of his charitable organizations The Prince's Foundation, has come under scrutiny following allegations that it has sold British citizenship to wealthy donors. the foundation is at present being investigated as part on an ongoing Metropolitan Police investigation into cash-for-honors accusations.

Chapter 1: The Early Years, Education And Family

Charles was born at Buckingham Palace at 9:14 p.m. on the 14th of November 1948. Being his first son of Elizabeth Duchess of Edinburgh and Philip Duke of Edinburgh He was born in the time of his grandparent's George VI. On the 15th of December, 1948 the baptized boy was blessed at the hands of the Archbishop from Canterbury, Geoffrey Fisher. Charles was named the heir apparent following the death of his grandfather as well as his queen's coronation Elizabeth II in 1952. As the monarch's oldest son, Charles immediately took on the titles Duke of Cornwall Duke of Rothesay Earl of Carrick Baron of Renfrew The Lord of The Isles, Prince and the Grand Steward of Scotland. Charles was also present at the coronation of his mother in Westminster Abbey on June 2 1953.

Catherine Peebles was selected to be in charge of his schooling and for three of his siblings Anne, Andrew, and Edward at Buckingham Palace, as was the norm for children from wealthy families. Charles is the very first the heir apparent to be educated this way and as Buckingham Palace stated in 1955 that he would go to school instead of having private tutors. Charles began his classes in the Hill House School in west London on the 7th of November 1956. Stuart Townend, the school's director, founder, and the school's headmaster did not show any favoritism by suggesting that the Queen Mother let Charles play football, as the kids were never friendly to any player on the field of football. Charles went on to attend his dad's two school: Cheam Preparatory School in Berkshire, England, commencing in 1958. He also attended Gordonstoun in northeast Scotland which began in April of 1962.

Elizabeth along with Philip are depicted as emotionally far from their parents, in the 1994 Jonathan Dimbleby official book about Prince Charles. Philip is accused of ignoring Charles's temperamental temperament and forcing Charles to go to Gordonstoun in which the school was a target for bullying. Although Charles was known to refer to the curriculum at Gordonstoun that is known for its rigor and rigor, being "difficult," the school "Colditz in kilts" Charles later expressed his admiration for Gordonstoun in a note that it given him "a significant amount about myself and my own strengths and weaknesses." It helped me be a leader and accept the challenges." In an interview in 1975 in 1975, he said the school felt "pleased" that he had been a part of Gordonstoun and said that his experience of the "toughness of the school" was "greatly exaggerated." The year was 1966. Charles was a student at the Timbertop campus at Geelong Grammar School in Victoria, Australia, for two months. He went across Papua New Guinea with his history teacher, Michael Collins Persse. Charles said at the time of his death that period in Timbertop has been the most enjoyable aspect that he had in the course of learning. After his return back to Gordonstoun, Charles followed in the footsteps of his father by becoming head boy. In 1967, he graduated, having 6 B-level GCE O-levels and two C level A-levels in the fields of history and French. When he was in his first year of school, Charles stated, "I was not as enthusiastic about school as I would have liked but I'm more content and happy at home more than any other place in the world."

Charles also broke with royal custom another time, when, following the completion of his A-levels and matriculating to university instead of joining in the British Armed Forces. In the month of October, 1967, he received a place to Trinity College, Cambridge, where he studied archaeology as well as anthrology for the first year of Tripos prior to switching to the field of historians for the next. The following term, Charles studied Welsh history as well as Welsh language at University College of Wales in Aberystwyth. He earned a 2:2 bachelor of Arts (BA) degree from the University of Cambridge on June 23, 1970. He was the first British inheritor to earn the degree of a university. Cambridge conferred him with an honorary Master of Arts (MA Cantab) degree on August 2nd 1975. The Master of Arts at Cambridge is an academic rank but not a postgraduate degree.

Prince of Wales

Charles was crowned the Prince of Wales and Earl of Chester on the 26th of July 1958, but the official ceremony of inauguration did not take place on July 1st, 1969 when his mother was crowned in Caernarfon Castle in a televised ceremony. Charles was admitted to into the House of

Lords in 1970 and made his first speech in June 1974. He was one of the princes to speak in this manner since the reigning monarchy of Edward VII in 1884. He made his speech again in 1975. Charles took on additional public duties and established the Prince's Trust in 1976 and traveling to America in 1981. United States in 1981. In the late 1970s, Charles was keen to serve as the Governor-General of Australia in the manner that Australian Premier Malcolm Fraser suggested. However, the idea was never implemented because of the lack of support from the public. Charles said, "So, what are you supposed to believe when you're willing to help but are told that you're not welcome?"

Training in the military and careers

Charles was a member of his time in the Royal Navy and Royal Air Force following in the tradition of his grandfather, father along with two other great-grandfathers. In his second year of studying at

Cambridge, he enquired and received instruction at the Royal Air Force, learning how to fly the Chipmunk plane in members of the Cambridge University Air Squadron. He flew to Air Force College Cranwell on March 8, 1971 to be trained as an air pilot. After the graduation ceremony held in September after which he was took a course of six weeks in Dartmouth, the Royal Naval College Dartmouth and began his career in the navy. Then he served on the guided missile destroyer HMS Norfolk from 1971 to 1972, and on the vessels HMS Minerva and HMS Jupiter from 1972 until 1973. (1974). in 1974. Charles was a pilot in a helicopter at RNAS Yeovilton, after which Charles joined his first unit, the 845 Naval Air Squadron, that was based within HMS Hermes. Following a crash landing in 1994 of the BAe 146 in Islay, where the crew was found negligent by an investigation panel He resigned his helicopter pilot license.

Charles took over the command of the minesweeper on the coast HMS Bronington on February 9 of 1976. It was the final 10 months of active service within the UK navy.

The official duties of Charles

The Daily Telegraph referred to Charles as the "most committed members of the family royal" in 2008. The year 2008 was when he was able to attend formal engagements of 560; in 2010 he was 499 and in 2011 there were nearly 600.

As the Prince of Wales, Charles performed official duties on behalf of the Queen. He officiated at investments and also attended funerals of foreign dignitaries. Charles frequently visited Wales in order to fulfill the requirements of a week during the summer months and taking part in important national occasions like the opening of the Senedd. Under his direction all six trustees from Royal Collection Trust met three times per year. Royal Collection Trust met three times each year.

In the year 1970, Charles traveled to Bermuda to mark its 350th year anniversary as Bermuda's Parliament. Bermuda Parliament. Additionally, Charles represented the Queen at the celebrations of independence in Fiji in the year 1970 as well as the Bahamas at the mid-1973 time, Papua New Guinea in 1975, Zimbabwe in 1980, and Brunei in 1984.

Christopher John Lewis, who was convicted of firing a.22-caliber round at her in 1981 tried to get out of a mental facility in 1983 and shoot Charles. Charles was on a trip to New Zealand with Diana and William. In protest to the dire situation of a number of hundred Cambodian asylum seekers held in detention facilities, David Kang fired two rounds with a starter pistol at Prince Charles while visiting Australia on Australia Day in January 1994. Charles is the very first member of the royal family to pay an official trip in Australia and the Republic of Ireland in 1995. The year 1997 was the first time Charles as well represented Queen Elizabeth II in the ceremony to hand over Hong Kong. In his speech, he read out the speech from Queen Elizabeth II to Hong people living in Hong Kong: "Britain is part of the history of Hong Kong, and Hong Kong is a part to the past of Britain. We are also committed to the future of one another ".

Charles revived the tradition in the form of his position as the Prince of Wales having an official harpist to promote Welsh musicians to play the harp, which is the national instrument played by Wales. Furthermore, he and Duchess of Cornwall are able to spend one week each year in Scotland and he acts as patron to various organisations. Being a part of the Canadian Armed Forces enables him to keep informed about the actions of troops and travel to them either in Canada or overseas to take part in celebrations. He laid a wreath at the Canadian Tomb of the Unknown Soldier made using French battlefield plants. Then, the following year, in 1981, he was an official patron for the Canadian Warplane Heritage Museum. In 2005, during the funeral service of Pope John Paul II, Prince Charles accidentally shook hands with the president of Zimbabwe, Robert Mugabe, who was sitting next to the Pope. Charles's office Charles released an announcement that read: "The Prince of Wales was shocked and was unable not to shake the hands of Mr. Mugabe. The Prince has a strong dislike for the current government in Zimbabwe. He has made contributions in the Zimbabwe Defence and Aid Fund which helps those who are who are oppressed by the government. Recently, the Prince visited Pius Ncube, the archbishop of Bulawayo and a fierce opposition to the government." The incident occurred in November of 2001 traveling on an official trip to Latvia Prince

Charles was hit on the face by an the adolescent Alina Lebedeva, who was armed with three red flowers.

In the year 2010, Charles also was Queen's representative at the The 2010 Commonwealth Games opening ceremony in Delhi, India. To show support for Commonwealth nations, Charles attends official events held in the United Kingdom, such as the Christchurch earthquake memorial ceremony held at Westminster Abbey in 2011. Between November 15 and 17th November 2013, he attended the debut Commonwealth Heads of Government Meeting in Colombo, Sri Lanka, as the Queen's representative.

As of 2013, Charles contributed an unknown sum of money in 2013 to The British Red Cross Syria Crisis campaign as well as the DEC Syria appeal, run by 14 British organisations that help Syrian civil conflict victims. As per The Guardian, Charles is believed to have given up his pension from the government to a fictitious charity which assists those who are elderly after reaching the age of 65 in 2013. in March of 2014, as a reaction to the spread of measles across Southeast Asia, Charles arranged for measles vaccinations of five million for children living in the Philippines. As per Clarence House, he was concerned by the news of the destruction caused by Typhoon Yolanda. Since 2004, he's been patron for International Health Partners, which gave the vaccinations that are expected to safeguard five million children who are under five years old from measles.

The so-called black-spider memos, sent by Charles to ministers during 2004 and in 2005 caused an embarrassment after an appeal by The Guardian newspaper to reveal the memos in accordance with the Freedom of Information Act of 2000. In the end, however, United Kingdom Supreme Court ruled in March 2015 that Charles's notes should be made public.

The Cabinet Office issued the letters on May 13th in 2015. When the memos were released and the responses were mostly positive and contained no critique of Charles. The media portrayed these memos to be "underwhelming" as well as "harmless" and stated that the release "backfired against those who tried to denigrate him," with a popular opinion also being favorable. In 2015, it was reported that Charles was able to access confidential UK cabinet papers.

In May of 2015, Charles and the Duchess of Cornwall took their first trip in the Republic of Ireland. The British Embassy in Ireland described the trip as a crucial step towards "promoting reconciliation and peace." While on the trip, Charles was seen shaking his hands at Galway in Galway with Gerry Adams, the leader of Sinn Fein. It is believed that he is the head of the IRA which is the terrorist group responsible for the murders of Charles family members. The media described the

Galway ceremony as a "historic handshaking" as well as an "important moment in the Anglo-Irish relationship." Prior to Charles's visit to Ireland, Two Irish political dissidents of the republic were arrested in connection with a plot to bomb. Semtex as well as rockets were found in the Dublin residence of Donal Coisdealbha, who was a self-styled glaigh the na hEireann group which was later found guilty and sentenced for five and five and a half years of prison. He was a part of an old-time Republican, Seamus McGrane of County Louth, who served 11.5 years in prison for being a member of the Real IRA.

Charles has been frequently in Saudi Arabia to promote weaponry exports for companies such as BAE Systems. From 2013 until 2015, he had a meeting in the presence of Mutab bin Abdullah who is Mutab bin Abdullah, the Saudi Arabian National Guard leader. In the Janariyah celebration in Riyadh in February 2014 the prince performed a traditional sword-dance along with people from the Saudi royal family. The same event also saw Prince Salman bin Abdulaziz was a benefactor to the British manufacturer of arms BAE Systems. Margaret Ferrier, a Scottish Member of Parliament, was critical of Charles in 2016 over his involvement in the sale of Typhoon combat aircrafts for sale to Saudi Arabia. Catherine Mayer, Charles's biographer and a Time journalist who claims to have talked to many sources within Charles's circle He says that Charles "doesn't enjoy being promoted as a weapon" in agreements that he has signed with Saudi Arabia and other Arab Gulf states. Mayer says the claim that Charles has only spoken out in his opposition to being used to promote weapons in private. In their meeting in 2018, Commonwealth chiefs of government decided that Charles will succeed Queen Elizabeth II as the Commonwealth Head. The head is selected and therefore is not an inheritance.

On 7 March 2019 on March 7, 2019, The Queen Elizabeth held a celebration held at Buckingham Palace to commemorate the 50th anniversary of Prince Charles his investiture as the Prince of Wales. Duchess of Cornwall the Duke and Duchess of Cambridge and Sussex as well as the Prime Minister Theresa May, and Welsh First Minister Mark Drakeford were attendees. In the same month on the request by the British government, Charles and Camilla traveled to Cuba for an official visit to Cuba, becoming one of the very first members of the British royalty to travel Cuba. The trip was seen as an effort to strengthen the ties to Cuba and the United Kingdom and Cuba.

In January of 2020 Charles was the very first British patron to the International Rescue Committee, an organization with the aim of helping help refugees and those who are displaced due to persecution, conflict or natural disasters. Charles issued an official statement in April 2021, in response to an increase in cases of COVID-19 in India and the announcement of the beginning of an emergency appeal to India through the British Asian Trust, of which he is the founding member. In the Oxygen to India campaign has helped purchase oxygen concentrators to hospitals that are in need.

On the 25th of March in 2020, it was revealed that Charles had contracted COVID-19 in the outbreak. Therefore, he and his wife were confined to their Birkhall home. Camilla has also underwent a test but the results came back not positive. In the words of Clarence House, he displayed "minor signs" however "remains in good health." They further explained, "It is impossible to discern from where Prince Charles contracted disease because of the amount of appearances that he's recently made." Charles as well as Camilla were tested quickly as a lot of NHS nurses, doctors and patients were not examined promptly. This was a source of criticism for several publications. In March of 2020 Clarence House stated that Prince Charles was recovering from the illness as well as no longer apprehensive after speaking to his physician. The next day in a video the prince declared that he will continue to live in social isolation.

A letter written by Charles in response to Governor-General Sir John Kerr after the removal of Australian Prime Minister Gough Whitlam in the year 1975 was published in the month of October in 2020 in the context of the compilation of correspondence between the palace regarding in 1975's Australian constitution crisis. in the correspondence, Charles appears to have backed Kerr's decisions. He wrote that the thing Kerr "did in the past was the right thing to do and the best choice and most Australians were in agreement with your decision when it came to it" and that he shouldn't be worried about "demonstrations and blunders" that resulted from his decision.

In November 2021 Charles was present at the celebrations marking Barbados's transition into the parliamentary republic, which eliminated the Queen from the position of the nation's chief of state. Charles received an invitation from the Prime Minister Mia Mottley to serve as the next leader of the Commonwealth which was the first time when a member of the royal family was able to witness the transition of a monarchy into republican government.

On the 10th of February 2022, the news was announced that Charles was tested positive again for COVID-19, and was unable to isolate himself. His wife then confirmed that she had contracted influenza. This was confirmed 10 days later by the queen. On February 20, 2021

Charles as well as his spouse were vaccinated against COVID-19.

He was present at his first State Opening of the UK Parliament in May 2022. He also gave the Mother's Speech on behalf of Queen Elizabeth for the first time as a state counsellor. The Times reported in June 2022 that Prince Charles privately criticized the UK government's Rwanda asylum program in a manner that was "appalling" as well as warned it could overshadow that June Commonwealth Heads of Government summit in Rwanda where he represented the Queen. Then, it was revealed the cabinet ministers had advised Charles to not make political comments because they believed that a constitutional crisis could arise should he continue to do so following his election as King.

The Prince's Trust: Philanthropy and charity

Since the establishment of the Prince's Trust in 1976, Charles has also founded 16 other charitable organizations. He currently is the head of each of them. Together, they comprise the Prince's Charities, which describes itself as "the largest multi-cause charity business within the United Kingdom (UK), with a budget of more than PS100 million each year and active in a broad range of fields such as youth and education as well as sustainable development, the built environment responsible business and enterprise and even international."

In the year 2010, Prince's Charities Canada was founded, much like its similar counterparts that is in United Kingdom. Additionally, Charles is the patron of over 400 other organisations and charities. Charles makes his travels across Canada to increase awareness of disabilities, youth as well as the environment, arts as well as medicine, elderly, the protection of culture and heritage, as well as education. Charles has contributed to causes that benefit the poor across Canada. He was a participant in The year 1998 International Day for the Elimination of Racial Discrimination celebrations with his sons. Charles has also founded the Melbourne the capital of Victoria, Prince's Charities Australia. It is expected that the Prince's Charities Australia will provide the coordination to Charles's charitable endeavors in Australia and around the world.

He was among the first leaders in the world to voice their concerns about the record of human rights violations by Romanian ruler Nicolae Ceausescu, sparking worldwide protests. Then, he joined his support for the FARA Foundation, a charity that assists abandoned and orphaned Romanian children.

Planning for urban areas as well as New Classical Architecture

Charles has been open about his opinions on urban and architectural planning. He pushed for the growth of New Classical Architecture and stated that Charles "cares deeply about issues like the urban environment and architecture, revitalization of inner cities, and the quality of living." In a speech that was delivered on the 30th of May, 1984 to commemorate an anniversary celebrating the 150th year of the Royal Institute of British Architects (RIBA) He described the proposed extension of the London National Gallery as a "Huge gigantic carbuncle that is on the back of a loved friend." He also criticised contemporary architecture's "glass blocks and towers of concrete." He also said that "it is feasible and essential from an individual's perspective to be respectful of old buildings street plans, street designs and traditional scales, but not being ashamed of admiring facades, ornaments or soft material." He also urged the community to participate in decisions about architecture and asked why don't be those specific curves and arches that convey emotions in the design? What's the issue? Why is everything to be straight, straight, and unbending as well as only at angles of right angle?

The book he wrote in 1987 and the BBC document A Vision of Britain were equally criticizing modern architecture. In spite of criticism from the press He continues to promote traditional urbanism, human scale and the preservation of older structures as well as sustainable design. Two of his charitable organizations eventually merged to form one charity) advocate for his beliefs. The Poundbury village Poundbury was built on land belonging to Cornwall's Duchy of Cornwall according to the plans of Leon Krier under the direction of Prince Charles and his principles.

In the wake of his resentment over the unchecked destruction in Canada's most historic urban centres in 1996, Charles was instrumental in the establishment of an official national trust for the built environment of Canada. He gave his Department of Canadian Heritage his assistance in the establishment of an organization that was modeled on the British National Trust; the concept was implemented by adopting the Canadian budget for the federal year 2007. The year 1999 was the first time Charles was willing to accept his name for his prize, the Prince of Wales Prize for Local Heritage Leadership, which the Heritage Canada Foundation presents to municipalities that have demonstrated an ongoing commitment to the preservation of the historic sites. In 2005, after traveling in his home in the United States and seeing the destruction caused by Katrina, he was struck by the destruction caused by Hurricane Katrina, Charles earned the National Building Museum's Vincent-Scully Prize for his achievements in architecture;

He gave $25,000 of the prize funds to help rebuild storm-damaged towns.

From 1997 onwards, Charles was a frequent visitor to Romania to witness and document the destruction of Orthodox monasteries as well as Transylvanian Saxon villages under Nicolae Ceausescu's communist regime. Charles is the most renowned patron of the Mihai Eminescu Trust which is a Romanian conservation and renewal organization and has bought a house in Romania. In 2006 the scholar Tom Gallagher stated in the Romanian newspaper Romania Libera that monarchists in Romania allegedly have offered Charles his Romanian throne. However, Buckingham Palace refuted these assertions. Charles has been a part of the creation of an area and a garden in the Oxford Centre for Islamic Studies that blends Islamic with Oxford architecture styles.

Charles has been known to intervene in projects involving functionalism and modernism. In 2009 Prince Charles wrote in response to Qatari royalty, the developer of the Chelsea Barracks site, in which he declared Lord Rogers plans of the location "unsuitable." Rogers was removed from the project as was the Foundation for the Built Environment was given the task of recommending the replacement. Rogers stated that the Prince intervened to block his plans to build Paternoster Square and the Royal Opera House. Royal Opera House and Paternoster Square. He criticized Charles's actions as "an misuse of authority" in addition to being "unconstitutional." Lord Foster, Zaha Hadid, Jacques Herzog, J. Nouvel, Renzo Piano as well as Frank Gehry, among others wrote a brief note addressed to The Sunday Times that the Prince's "private remarks" as well as "behind-the-scenes lobbying" hindered an "open and democratic process of planning." In a letter sent directed to RIBA,

Piers Gough and other architects decried Charles's ideas for being "elitist" and advised colleagues to refrain from attending his speech. The developer of the project, CPC Group, filed an action against Qatari Diar in the High Court and was deemed Charles involvement "unwelcome." When the case was settled in the court, the CPC Group offered its apology "for any harm that was caused by their choosing to file a lawsuit at Qatari Diar and the claims that were made by CPC during the hearing."

Following the disastrous 2010 Haiti earthquake After the earthquake in Haiti, the Prince's Foundation for the Built Environment was able to aid in the reconstruction and renovation of buildings within Port-au-Prince, Haiti. The restoration of historic constructions within Kabul, Afghanistan, and Kingston, Jamaica, is an important aspect of the foundation. The project is called the foundation's Prince's Fund for the Built Environment's "greatest task to date." He was awarded the Driehaus Architecture Prize for patronage in 2012 in recognition of his work as a patron for New Classical Architecture. The University of Notre Dame's prize is considered to be the most highly coveted award for New Classical Architecture and urban planning.

The commitments of the Livery company

Charles was named an Honorary Liveryman in the Worshipful Company of Carpenters "in recognition of his passion for the architecture of London." Furthermore, Charles is a Permanent Master of the Worshipful Company of Shipwrights, Freeman from the Worshipful Company of Drapers, Freeman from the Worshipful Company of Musicians, and a member of the Company of Goldsmiths, and a great Liveryman for the Worshipful Company of Gardeners.

Chapter 2: "A King Waiting To Be King"

Prince Charles sent an condolence message to inhabitants who live in Antigua, Barbuda, Anguilla and other Caribbean islands following the devastation of the hurricane Irma.

He wrote"My wife and I felt so sad to hear about the terrible loss of life and the complete destruction caused by the massive storm.'

Then he offers his support and sympathy to those who have suffered the devastating natural catastrophe.

A few days prior to the date of this message the couple, along with his wife Duchess of Cornwall attended a funeral held at Westminster Abbey.

This was done to commemorate the anniversary of the Battle of Britain.

They joined the remaining people who survived the Battle for the memorial service. One, 96-year old Squadron Leader Geoffrey Wellum was moved close to tears.

Prince Charles talked with the veteran of war, and is also an active war heroand one of the few remaining members of The Few (the nickname taken from Churchill's famous speech).

Wellum was a participant in a conflict that ended only a few months before Charles the birth of Charles.

A few days before the Westminster Abbey event, he gave honor, for the very first time at The Westmoreland County Show, which was established in 1799. In 1799, George III was the monarch.

Before this prior to that, the Prince as well as his spouse also took part in a tour of Scotland and Scotland, as well as other things, which included dancing to the music by the Elvis impersonator, and the launch of a vessel, which was named (appropriately appropriately) The Prince of Wales... The Prince of Wales also held a garden celebration as well as a visit to a stately house in Edinburgh, visited children and community groups, and so and on.

All of this over just two weeks. This is for a man who's aged 68. Yet, he is not King.

He's in a time that the majority of people are aging, and becoming retired, but to him, the most difficult task is still ahead. Of course, the day when he'll became the King of Britain and the Commonwealth.

In addition to the activities mentioned above, in every single one of them he's present, viewed and scrutinized for any slight slip within the span of a normal month, he's performed the following tasks:

He's been welcoming President Obama Irish President at Dumfries House. He also was at a concert to celebrate the 25th anniversary of FM classic.

He is involved in the preparation of a trip to Malta that will be held at the end of this year. He has hosted events and met with officials as well as residents of the community. He has assumed some of the responsibilities of his now old mother and father who recently retired.

There are also the overseas commitments of his mother and a large portion the parents' charity obligations. It's not an easy to live a life for someone of his age.

He is responsible for the 13 charities he founded himself that help good causes throughout the Commonwealth.

They also include some that aren't huge for example, like for instance, the Royal Drawing School, which offers art instruction to deserving students.

Also, important institutions like The Prince's Regeneration Trust, which helps to ensure the protection of old structures.

He is the head of The British Asian Trust, which provides assistance to local charities across a variety of parts of the continent including India, Pakistan, Bangladesh and Sri Lanka.

It also helps Asian charity organizations in it's United Kingdom. The man is the spokesperson for more than 400 charitable organizations of one type or another.

As the Queen is taking a break from her duties, the king has entertained over 6000 guests per year at events held at different royal residences.

He travels a minimum of 100000 miles per year during overseas trips visiting celebrities, shaking hands with crowds of admirers and rallying troops far from their home.

As of this writing this article, he's 68 years old and almost 69 and for only three of them he has awakened to the fact that in the event that his mother died unexpectedly, he'd be the king.

She has also been an avid horse rider but she does not wear an helmet. The threat of a terror attack is always been there.

There was always the chance that a deranged person could attack and kill her. Any time it was possible that he would have become the king.

Should the choice to abdicate be taken by the king, he will take the throne.

However, it hasn't happened. We are confident that the Queen remains in well-being and health. Her conviction in the duties of Monarchy means that there is no sign that she is going to abdicate.

The degree to which he would like to assume the role is a matter of debate. The son of his father, Prince Harry, recently expressed his displeasure that Royals are faced with the possibility of being able to assume the title of Monarch.

If his desire to assume the role is incomplete, insignificant or not even present We can be certain that, should duty call that of Prince Charles will try his best to meet his obligations.

An Heirloom is born

Prince Charles was born and resided at Buckingham Palace for the first eight months of his life. He later relocated together with his parents into Clarence House, which would later be the home of his grandmother.

When he was born at the age of two, he was second in line to the throne following his mother.

Anne, his younger sister Anne who was also born shortly after in the year 1950.

The Prince was raised in the traditional royal family. The world was going through postwar transformation, yet the monarchy believed that its role to protect the status quo by providing stability in the midst that was a time of uncertainty.

World War Two had recently been declared over. Britain was a country that was still suffering from rationing and bomb sites dotted the major cities and towns. In the Soviet Union already threatened uncertain futures.

Many families lost their family members and friends during the war. Peace was wonderful, however the people still suffered. The uncertain times was evident in the time Churchill was the person who was the man who led Britain to victory against the evils and evil of Hitler as well as the Nazi Party, was deposed as the Prime Minister.

In these times of turmoil The Queen believed that her main duty was to the nation. That was also the message that she got from her advisers.

Charles was raised by two Nannies. Charles was extremely loved, and still is of one, but of the other knowing that she was sacked for rescheduling a dessert requested by the Queen for her son speaks volumes.

The nanny was a popular subject for the nickname "No-nonsense Lightbody'. It's enough said.

Helen Lightbody, who never got married, was the daughter of an Scottish textile worker. She also was the head of the royal nursery for eight years between 1948 and 1956.

But Charles kept in contact with his mentor and she was even a guest at his investiture in 1969 as the Prince of Wales at the age of 21 years old.

She died in 1987.

His relationship with his other Nanny (who also took care of his children) was significantly closer.

She was still requested to represent the royals at certain occasions until recently, and was also invited to be part of the royal family on an exclusive cruise in the time she reached her early 80s.

It was to celebrate the significant births for Prince Anne (who is at the age of sixty) in addition to Prince Andrew who was turning fifty.

The Prince keeps in contact with the person who has a special place in his life. is considered a his mentor and friend.

Charles was only three years old when he was made heir to the throne. His Grandfather King George VI, dies. The death of his father was and if it wasn't exactly what was planned, definitely not unexpected.

After this The Queen Mother was to later become the third significant influence on his life, because she spent a lot of time caring for the child as his mother tended to her duties in the world of civic and international.

The bond with the queen Mother with Prince Charles will always be extremely close.

Indeed, this attitude to motherhood by her is one we'll return to in the future. It influenced Charles into a similar manner towards his sons that was countered through his former wife Diana, his first wife. Diana. Also, a warm personality that Charles naturally has.

These sons are now aware of that parents are important to being present with their children. Prince William will do his best, as much as is feasible to accomplish this with his own children.

We should not be snarky about her for having been absent from young Charles his life. She was young and was surrounded by people who believed that the idea of "Monarchy" was more important than any obligation of the other'm motherhood'.

Being a mom is a time of emotions that are beyond the control of the mother, and by putting duties as the highest priority on her list of priorities the Queen may have been suffering emotionally because she was absent from her son.

It was just the way of the world, and she should be appreciated, not condemned for her choices. It is not a good idea to judge by the current perspective.

When he was just three, Charles gained more titles than just being the heir to throne. He became the Duke of Cornwall following the demise of his father.

The other side of United Kingdom was further recognized by the titles given to the child, to who they could have been little at the time.

He was made Duke of Rothesay and Earl of Carrick Baron of Renfrew Lord of the Isles and Great Steward and Prince of Scotland.

at the age of 4 and quarter, the Prince of Wales and holder of many titles was present at the coronation of his mother at Westminster Abbey. He was in the same seat as his aunt and grandmother princess Margaret.

The Queen chose a Governess as her son, who was her eldest. Catherine Peebles was another Scot and they were a good match. Charles would refer to her as Bambi.

However, although Charles loved learning in his early years but he was also easily distracted The Queen also did show an aversion to tradition. Instead of choosing an individual tutor, Charles became the first heir of the throne who attended the school.

Evidently, this wouldn't be a school that is attended by the vast majority of children his age. He was a part of a traditional, all-boys school in London.

Hill House included 'marching' in its syllabus It appears that the young Prince did well in school.

But his time there at Hill House was brief. The father of his son, Prince Phillip, had been a student at a privately-owned all-boys boarding school known as Cheam located near Newbury.

It's the ideal school for the prince of the future who will follow his father's steps.

The eight-year-old, however, was not a fan of boarding and was suffering from severe home-sickness. In a short time, the issues got so bad that Queen wrote to then Premier Minister Anthony Eden, saying:

"Charles is getting ready to be anxious about returning for school this week. even more so for the next term.'

For a nine-year-old child to be taken from everything he knew to what were at the time times extremely harsh institutions that were dominated by males it's not likely that he would be unsatisfied. It is not surprising that he was all on his own.

Aside from his frequently missing parents main individuals in his existence been up until then the Governess of his home along with his nannies grandmother and his sibling. All women.

However, Charles finally settled down down, and found comfort in getting involved in drama at school and sports. Perhaps predictably, he was named Head Boy during his last year.

Cheam School of today Cheam School of today is quite different from the one of Prince Charles at the time of Prince

Charles. Children are taken care of and are content. The school is the majority of boarders. Parents are welcomed, and enjoy much more contact with their children.

The issue of Prince Charles his secondary school started to rear its head in the final portion of his time at Cheam.

Eton College was the choice of his grandmother. Naturally that, as a college, it is a major institution with a global fame.

Today, it's an innovative school where pedagogy and privilege are combined. It also helps numerous boys whose families might not be in a position to afford the school that is offered.

In the late fifties and the early sixties, just like the majority of Public Schools, it was difficult to get into, and the children of the wealthy could be found swimming or lying in the midst of their fellow students.

One of the things that attracted her for The Queen Mother is the fact that the school was located right across the River from Windsor which is which is where there is also the Royal Castle is to be located.

London is just a brief journey away.

The school that was chosen for the young Prince could not have been further away.

Gordonstoun was, just like Cheam the school that Prince Phillip had attended. The school was actually started by a cousin of his.

The school is located in north Scotland located in Moray, Gordonstoun made the likes of Cheam and Eton appear to be holiday camps. For Phillip who was a tough guy with an impressive personality and the ability to care for him, his school might be a good fit.

For his son, who was sensitive and a little unsure It was hell.

Prince Charles hated the place. Never shy in the face of truth, the prince reportedly told his parents back then (as Cheam did with Cheam) in the past and was very out about his dislike for the school since then.

The Prince was brutally and savagely bullied. A English child of the royal family would always be the center of attention in an institution, however the circumstances at school could not be accepted today.

The weather was cold and rainy every day and, despite being in the frigid Scottish region the shorts were worn all throughout the year.

Charles was able to get through the time. He was the first monarch to take public exams. At at the age of sixteen He was able to pass O level with English languages, English Literature, Latin, French, History and Maths.

The Prince's two final years of schooling were divided in Australia as well as Scotland. He attended The Timbertop School, which like English public schools, put a the highest importance on physical activity.

He returned, this time as Head Boy at Gordonstoun to complete his A-levels. Being Head Boy meant that he would not have to share a dormitory because a single room was the privilege of the post.

Charles was able to pass A levels with distinction in History and French and received A and a C grade, respectively. Charles was the first royal of the House of Windsor to earn official educational credentials.

In the classroom, however another small signal to suggest that monarchies were moving towards the door that was closed to modernization came to light.

The expected next step for the future heir to the throne was to be joining the military. However, Charles did not follow this path.

Chapter 3: A Modern (Ish) Young Man

A route Prince Charles took nearly led to a shift in British history as well as the foreshortening of the book on his life.

He was riding his bicycle in his time in Trinity College, Cambridge, during which an altercation took place. The details of the incident were kept in the background however Prince Charles took part in a close-shave with an unidentified bus.

A battle that he wouldn't be likely to win.

The Prince's grandfather, George VI, had spent a full year at Trinity where he studied the history of economics, civics, and politics.

But, Charles planned to stay on the path, and finish with a good grade.

The first year of his life which began with the month of October in 1967 devoted to the research into archaeology, as well as physical and social Anthropology.

He was able to spend two months of the next year studying archeological sites in France and participated in diggings in Jersey. He graduated with a 2:1 grade at the beginning of his first year.

When he was set to be crowned the Prince of Wales and Prince of Wales, he was a student at Aberystwyth University on the Welsh coast where he was able to study the Welsh language and its history after which he returned to Trinity.

He changed to History while back in Cambridge and eventually secured an impressive 2:2. The student life can be a fantastic experience for students which is why Charles was no exception.

He was active in the drama club of his university in the form of a variety of roles in different productions. As a prelude to his future desire to be politically active, particularly when the environment was involved, he participated during an Cambridge Union debated.

What's the issue? This house believes that technological advances threaten the human spirit and is making him a slave.'

Though the man said he was neutral about the issue and said, 'I'm in a somewhat difficult spot in my position,' he stated that he was able to make his opinions explicit by mentioning the potential for pollution and the doubtful value of certain technological advancements.

However, the royal obligations also impacted the opportunities to pursue studies. He was crowned the Prince of Wales by the Queen in the summer of 1969.

He was part of an extensive tour of New Zealand, Australia and Japan. He was a guest at the State Opening of Parliament, was officially introduced to the House of Lords and attended Privy Council meetings.

It's interesting to examine his experiences in comparison to the experiences of his son William during his time in University. While Charles continued to fulfill his obligations, and participated in what could have been an overwhelmingly political-motivated event within Wales, William was tucked in a quiet corner in St Andrew's University, in an isolated part of Scotland.

In the school, he was nearly solely allowed to concentrate on his studies and also enjoy the life of an undergraduate.

The media was keen in the relationship between William and Kate Middleton, of his research, very little was made public.

The royal duties were guaranteed to not impair his studies.

But, things changed in the 1960s and into the 1970s. It was all about duty and Charles had to work with his studies at college.

After the university, stints with the military took up the majority of the time for the young man. The first was an eight-month stint with the Royal Air Force in Cranwell, Lincolnshire.

The pilot was already certified pilot and had studied to be able in flying jets. As a Air Lieutenant, he received wings at the close of the summer of 1971.

Then, he was able to spend an experience in the Navy in which he was promoted to the rank of acting Sub Lieutenant.

His journey began with Dartmouth College, and once again, he was following the footsteps of his father. Also, the footsteps of his uncle Lord Mountbatten.

The two were extremely close and we'll explore their relationship in greater detail later on.

After a few months in Dartmouth after which he joined the crew of HMS Norfolk, which was a destroyer in the area of Gibraltar.

In the following thirty-months He served on four additional vessels, including tours of the Pacific in which He was stationed on the frigate named HMS Jupiter.

After that, his love for flying was further rewarded when he enrolled in a course to become an Helicopter flyer. He also was pilot on the ship HMS Hermes.

He was further trained, and was later assigned the command over HMS Bronington, a mine hunter.

Even though he quit the military as a active serviceman in the year 1976 it is not impossible to get promotions. In addition to many honourary distinctions, he currently has a rank of five stars across all three military services: air force, navy and army.

It's a reflection on his time, sway of the monarchy's access during that time and the formality of The Queen , which is why has been largely ignored about his period at University as well as during his time in the Army.

In relation to their sons we have many more details about what they are up to. There is a good chance that William was a quiet eater in St Andrews, we know that the family he was living with was Kate who lived in a home with three other people.

This is in a scenario when the media was willing to allow the boys to go to peace.

We have heard about Harry's experiences as a soldier. We also know of his experiences being deployed in war zones and other similar situations.

The media's interest in Charles at the time was substantial, but not comparable to what it is today.

But that, however, was to alter. Prince Charles was released from the military and became the world's most attractive bachelor.

Romance In The Air

Charles uncle, Lord Mountbatten, offered some suggestions to his nephew on the subject of love and romance.

Perhaps it wasn't not politically correct However, he did suggest"In a scenario similar to yours, a man should plant his wild oats and engage in as many relationships as could before getting settled.

"But for a wife, you should pick a good pretty, attractive, and sweet girl before meeting someone else she may be attracted to.

It is a traumatic experience to women's lives,' the doctor added to have experiences when they remain in a position of honor after marriage.'

The specifics of what these experiences might have been the subject of his discussion, but he didn't specify.

Also the Viceroy who was once in charge of India was suggesting that Charles should take a trip and enjoy the time of his life, and then choose (a one-way choice?) an unworldly, innocent woman to marry.

The liberation of women in the latter half of the sixties, and into the early seventies did not go beyond that of the Royal family.

One of of these ladies who was eligible is, we are aware, a woman who's long-lasting love would be a part of his entire life.

This lady was not in Lord Mountbatten's definition of the ideal woman for the throne of the future, and it was a mix of the Palace as well as his family and Charles his own perception that he was doing the right thing, ruled her out during the era in the 1970s.

This is Camilla the wife of his current husband. We will discuss the relationship in greater depth later.

It is nevertheless worth observing how far removed from the other people of Britain as well as how far from the current attitudes the Royal family had the days.

It was the 1960s and the early 1970s, which was a period of the hippie movement and free love, as well as flower power. It was the time of The Beatles as well as The Rolling Stones.

Here is a young man being told to get his flings and then choose a woman to marry in the same way that we can choose a certain chocolate bar from vending machines.

Them and Us were never the same.

As the heir to the throne, he was a great choice for a young upwardly-oriented girl, perhaps with parents who were ambitious.

However, the emotions of the prince's younger self appeared to be a distant second to the idea of what would constitute an appropriate wedding for him.

It wasn't only his family who felt that he had to act in accordance with what was considered right.

The dark figures in the background who, during the past, made sure that the monarchy was viewed in the way they believed they should view it. desired a 'proper' wedding for Charles.

The public, too would like to see a couple get married by their own love.

The public's opinions were an important factor. Some people - particularly those of a certain age - felt happy with the new generation of youth that was gaining strength in the era of the time.

Many youngsters are growing their hair or experimenting with drug culture as well as living in sin and all that however, their parents' generation who had been through and participated in World War II, felt differently.

They were looking for a future king who could have a romantic life an environment that they would be happy.

A young man who was already married and had found the love of his life being tossed around by such a way been nearly unbearable at times.

A good marriage means in the real world there were two options. The bride must either meet (or have found) the princess of another country, or marry a member of the Aristocracy.

This narrowed the field to a certain extent.

But, he tried his best to be following the advice of his uncle who was his most beloved, by'sowing wild Oats.'

First According to the majority of sources she was the daughter of the Chilean ambassador Lucia Santa Cruz. Also, she was the master and research associate at Trinity College while Charles was studying at the University.

The relationship between the two blossomed in the year 1968 and it lasted over two decades. They have been friends and she was even invited to his wedding with Camilla Parker Bowles.

The press might be a bit more reserved than it is now, and it certainly was during the time of the Prince's romance to Diana Spencer. However, the press still enjoyed the idea of a good story.

In the modern world, Charles would have been called 'ripped' in his 20s, and coupled with the title of Prince of Wales and the title Prince of Wales, he was an attractive choice for many women.

It might be more of a matter of the two choosing him rather than the reverse.

The press reported that he appeared reports, to be a part of a group of prominent names from the arts world. Even though they give nothing more than warm and kind remarks about Charles and do not reveal any more information (if there's any) the actor was connected to the actress Susan George and Three Degrees singer Sheila Ferguson.

A royal family getting married to an African-American woman in the 1970s could be truly ground-breaking and something that officials should have tried to avoid.

While serving in the military on HMS Jupiter the ship, he made a stop in San Diego. There the crew was introduced to Laura Jo Watkins.

A welcome party was organized for Charles as well as US Admiral Watkins was invited however, he was unable to attend. His daughter Laura instead. They were in contact for a few times, but Charles was to become the Head of the Church of England, and the Watkins family were Catholics.

And the palace couldn't permit that. It could have been Henry VIII all over again. The press would be having an entire day of action.

Following, at the time he was Captain of HMS Bonnington, he dated Janet Jenkins, who was a receptionist in the British Consulate in Montreal.

Their love affair was one that they attempted to keep private. Similar to other romances, this one lasted as a relationship after any relationship ended.

Letters between the couple surfaced in 2009 on eBay during 2009 and several instances offered more than an idea of the relationship to the pair.

One letter suggest a romantic date in which he writes 'I'd have believed your home was the most peaceful', and in a different one, he apologizes that he is sorry to have to hurry away, ruining a cozy evening.'

A variety of queens were spotted. One of them was Sibylla Dorman, child of the governor of Malta. Lady Jane Grosvenor, who was daughter of the Duke of Westminster.

The other daughter of Lady Camilla Fane who was the daughter of Earl of Westmorland and was also the Queen's master of horses.

The pattern is starting to emerge. Famous aristocratic fathers and daughters at the appropriate age. Some of them include Lady Angela Nevill (daughter of Prince Phillip's secretary).

Cindy Buxton was a career woman, yet still of the aristocratic lineage Her dad was Lord Buxton from Alsa. Jane Wellesley worked for the BBC and Her father was Duke of Wellington.

Lady Henrietta Fitzroy (daughter to the Duke of Grafton) was a daughter of the Duke of Grafton. She had a mother near to the Royal family. She was the queen's lover of the robes.

Of course this was the kind of circle that Charles movedaround, therefore it's inevitable that he'd meet the most beautiful young ladies.

The number of relationships he had in such a short amount of time suggests that his soul was somewhere else.

He could have become attracted to these aristocratic people however, the impression seems been created from the fact that it's more about helping find the perfect spouse than true, genuine affection.

It was, already in Charles's heart it was meant to Camilla Shand.

One of the daughters from the Aristocracy that he encountered had a father who bore the title of 'Earl' Spencer'. She grew up near the queen's Sandringham retreat, and been in contact with Charles many times as they were in the midst of growing.

Sarah Spencer had a younger sister named Diana who, from the time she was in her teens, had an itch to meet the Prince more.

Then she would achieve her goals.

However, let's go back to the list of possible lovers who Charles was given. One woman who seemed to fulfill the requirements would be Davina Sheffield. Davina Sheffield.

She and Charles began to meet in the late 70s and she appeared to have all the qualities that the palace was looking for in a prospective bride. She was a descendant of a noble family Her grandfather was Lord McGowan beauty, elegance and a love of the prince.

It was revealed that she also lived in an era of sin' with her former lover, who did not disclose the truth. That's not something you would happen, so another one was a victim of the sand.

Sabrina Guinness, a member of the brewing family could have been a famous wife. She was a lover of Mick Jagger, Rod Stewart and actor Jack Nicholson by the time the relationship began together with Prince Charles in 1979.

But she wasn't Prince Phillip's favorite, and he was a bit snobby after Charles offered to take her to Balmoral.

He was gently pushed toward Lord Mountbatten's granddaughter, Amanda Knatchbull.

In actual fact she was quite young and still a teenager at the time that Charles like an adult gentleman sent a letter to her mother in order to announce his desire.

While the reaction received was mostly positive, the mother was of the opinion she was in the moment, far too young to begin a relationship of this magnitude. an opulent relationship.

In the future, Charles would propose to her, but she would reject her down.

Anna Wallace was his final relationship before he started to meet Diana. The name was coined for her due to her fiery personality and active hunting, Prince Charles also proposed to Diana.

In an event in a palace, the man left her. And she was not pleased with the decision, so they ended their relationship by saying:

"You've let me go for the entire evening, and now you'll need to go on in my absence.'

There was a beautiful, young blonde girl, the daughter of a former partner. However, it wasn't Diana who was distracting the Prince all evening.

It was not his real passion, Camilla.

Chapter 4: Controversy

Charles is an individual who hasn't always been a popular choice for our politicians.

Beware of any possibility of gaining favor with the general public they haven't enjoyed the prince's intervention in areas they believe that he ought to leave alone.

His writings are referred to as the 'black spider words due to the handwriting style he wrote in.

Their content, however, has been criticized as typically more black widow rather than garden spider. But this is an oxymoron. It was perhaps a way to gain points on the political side against a Prince who was frequently unpopular with the general public.

However the letters, a few of which are available in the public domain are usually polite and well-written. One of them begins at the risk of becoming an absolute bore ...'

However when the letters come from the one who is the heir to the crown they have more weight than a letter from Miss Smith further down the road.

Traditionally, the role of the monarch in politics is strictly ceremonial. Even though the Queen is still allowed to read red boxes (which include ministerial documents) and, theoretically, is in charge of approving every law but she is not allowed to take part in politics.

She may be able to provide some calming influence, maybe for the more risk-averse politicians - she did not get along to Tony Blair, according to reports - but that's the extent of her influence.

In the event that prince Charles sends letters to Ministers as well as other decision makers the person he writes to is in the capacity of a private person.

However, he is part of the royal family, an heir to the throne, and the fact that his position could influence decisions can't be ignored.

Charles who has been described as a meddling prince', has some areas on which he's very vocal.

A passionate man, he is interested in agriculture the genetic modification process, designing and architecture. He is also who is concerned about the effects of social inequality and global warming.

It is not, as we have to conclusively, the subjects which are controversial. Sure, most right-thinking folks are concerned about global warming and the unnoticed effects of genetic modification.

We may not be unless there is a politician who is out for a gain or an untrustworthy businessman. (Or maybe, in the case of global warming is involved or the president of a large manufacturing nation).

Rumours, such as the Prince's use of ink in the color green to emphasize the points or to rant about politics are not particularly evident.

But only the letters from 2005 were published. This was in response to an FOI request made by Guardian newspaper.

The Establishment was adamant against the publication of the letters, and even took the matter up to Court of Appeal, however they were judged as being in the public's interest.

But, after the story was in the news The Government enacted changes in the Freedom of Information Act, meaning that no further correspondence will be made public for at least twenty-five years or five years following when the Prince dies.

It could be because there's some aspect of the letter that's truly controversial. Also, it is possible or not, it's just aspect of the ongoing state of nanny-state that decides what's appropriate and not for citizens to be aware of.

We will probably discover the truth within the next 20 years or so.

An ex-deputy private secretary who was also the adviser for Prince of Wales Prince of Wales is quite clear that the letters are controversial.

in 2006 Mark Bolland, offered his opinions on the subject of the missives.

He said that the prince was "dissident" and tried to challenge the dominant politics.

Bolland was appointed to the Prince's advisory council after the passing of the Princess Diana. The Prince's personal score had decreased to only 20 percent in the year 2000 Bolland's primary responsibility was to fix that.

He was extremely successful and the approval rating of the Prince was significantly higher, reaching an average of mid-seventies.

Bolland also played a role in helping to bring stories of his romance with Camilla to the public domain. He also was adamant about keeping William and Harry's privacy throughout their education.

However, Bolland who was an Canadian was not always liked by the larger group of advisors at the palace. In 2002 an additional official named Michael Peat, was recruited.

The two bonded well on a personal basis however, they had their own goals. There were professional issues and Bolland began to move on, setting up his own PR company.

But, despite his strong backing of the Prince he didn't pull any punches about the black spider's letters.

He claimed that the prince frequently interfered in political affairs and did not just write letters. He also scheduled meetings with ministers and communicated with leaders in and outside of the world of politics.

Bolland claimed Bolland said that Charles was neither political, but was active. Contrary to what was found in the 2005 studies Bolland said Charles's letters are very extreme.

Bolland would often, as claimed by Bolland at times, he would criticize those in other nations in the strongest possible terms.

In 2002, a document was released by the palace in connection with Charles his letters. The statement said that Charles' letters were not addressed to him.

'...takes the active part in every aspect of British life. He believes that in addition to celebrating successes, one of his responsibilities should be to bring out the problems and present views that are at risk of being overlooked.

This role will only be performed properly when complete confidentiality is maintained.

It is proper and right to have an interest to British daily life.'

Ummm.

Everyone, of course have the right to voice our opinions. If they're part from Joe Public, they carry only a small amount of influence.

If they come from a prominent person, they can generate press curiosity.

Other than when it's an official member of the royal family.

There's a certain realism in this quote of having a cake in your mouth and eating it alone as well as in one's own private home.

One particular intervention has caused a tense debate. The controversy has been dubbed the Cumbrian farmer's letter.

The letter was addressed to then-Prime Premier Tony Blair, and its leak was a part of the 'Liberty and Livelihood' protest held by the Countryside Alliance.

The group is one whom Charles would be willing to join, but Tony Blair would not. Within the letters, Charles is adamant about the opinions of the Cumbrian farmer.

These aren't views that are a sign of wisdom, however fervent they might be.

A letter from the farm owner writes that: "If the majority of us, as a whole were gay, black or black, we would not be a victim or slammed.'

Charles added that rural communities would receive greater assurances from Government in the event that they were part of the other minorities.

It's not known who leaked the email. The Conservative MEP, Nicholas Soames, had his name in the image, however, he did not deny any involvement.

As did Number 10. What can be said to be an conclusion is that the Office of the Prime Minister was known for its transparency and spin whenever it was in their favor was the one with the most to gain.

Even in 2002, the majority of people would be shocked at the Cumbrian farmer's comments in relation to homosexual and black minorities.

The Prince's association with the view of the people increased the significance of the story. (we are certain that the reason was his love for the minorities that are rural rather than any harm he intended for others minorities).

It could also deflect media attention focused on the protests.

Chapter 5: Family Matters

The connection that binds Charles and his mother began at a very early age. The bond would not be broken until the time of her death in 2002.

He told me, when she passed away she was a person who meant everything to me and I had always was terrified of this moment. In some way, I didn't think it would be here. She appeared to be utterly invincible.'

He added that his "darling, magic grandmother's always seen the humorous side of life and that they laughed until they hurt.

"O, how I will regret her smile and her wonderful wisdom.' He said"Ever when I was just a young child I loved her.'

Remember that she was the one who grew him up with his nannies while the parents went away. She tried to unsuccessfully convince them to choose the nearby Eton College when she knew that a far away Gordonstoun was not the best choice for him.

She wrote to Queen Elizabeth II her Lillibet in the year 1961, writing that she was hoping he would enter Eton and that, if he did, it would be a happy time with his fellow students there.

Furthermore, she could monitor her father and visit him often.

As per her biographer Hugo Vickers, the Queen Mother observed aspects of her spouse in Charles. An insecurity that suggested an individual who needed lots of help, and needed to be boosted up.

As George VI was in need of to be throne when his brother had abdicated.

He was not responding she was sure, to the sort of'man who was a toughening-up of the sort Prince Phillip, however well in his heart, was sure to receive from his school of study.

In reality, while the time came, Charles would often visit his mother in his grandmother's Scottish residence, Birkhall. In the home, he would express his feelings of loneliness, homesickness and the struggles that a prince faced in getting settled into school when as compared to the other boys.

These fears will, naturally, be a problem for Charles throughout his adulthood. These fears could be at the root of his inability to defend himself as well as Camilla at the time they first wanted to get married.

Insecurity which led him to heed the advice from palace official in a manner that seemed apathetic in the face of his deep sadness by the loss of his marriage, his "Greek Tragedy" in the manner he described it.

Many people who have worked closely with royals claim that today, Charles (along with Camilla) are the most straightforward of all royals to work with.

However, this was not always the scenario. Some have reported of anger-filled eruptions of anger - that of an anxious, depressed man.

When he was with his dear grandmother, life was much more fun, easier and enjoyable. It was her passion for culture that instilled in Charles numerous of the things which he is most passionate about.

She would accompany him to ballet and show him the artworks at Windsor Castle, explaining their significance.

Up until her death she kept a photograph showing Charles as a child on her desk. Also, her numerous letters clearly show how much she loved Charles.

Charles was evidently her favorite She writes in a letter after an appendix operation saying that she was told by the queen along with Prince Andrew have visited her however she writes"I really wish that the door would be opened and that you were there!

It was clear that the relationship between Queen Mary and Diana was not the best. It was mainly related to being aware that Charles was not happy in the relationship. She wasn't openly hostile but rather ignored her.

He erected a memorial for her following her passing, and then he declared: "I am so sad for my grandmother every day.'

Another extremely close connection Charles had with one of his family members was his respect and love to his great uncle, Lord Mountbatten.

He referred to the leader of the military as his grandfather in honor. Should the Queen Mother gave him a shoulder which Charles could vent his pain, Mountbatten would offer counsel.

He played an important role in the matchmaking romance between the princess Elizabeth with Prince Philip who was from Greece. Then he returned and was responsible for introducing Charles to his daughter.

The man also gave Charles the use of his home in order to be free of any media attention.

Mountbatten recommended that Charles find a wife who was 'free of an past'. He certainly did that by marrying Lady Diana.

Lord Mountbatten was killed when he was boating on a lake close to his summer residence in Ireland. The IRA acknowledged responsibility for the death of not just Lord Mountbatten but also his 14-year-old grandson, a 15-year-old boatman, and an 82-year-old Dowager Lady Brabourne.

Some years later Charles was able to make a visit to the place of the death of his beloved uncle. He spoke of the immense grief that he felt at the loss.

The relationship between the Prince and his siblings has evolved in the course of time. As a young boy and male, he was no doubt a loving cousin and father to Anne, Andrew and Edward.

However, their lives have diverged over years. The pressure of becoming an heir to the vast wealth generated by Duchy of Cornwall, the pressure to be heir

Duchy of Cornwall and the magnitude of the decline and the rebirth of Charles have led to the fact that Charles' life has been in many ways distinct from that of his siblings and brothers.

Certain, Edward apart, each has had to go through the breakup of a relationship, however Charles was far more scrutinised and drawn out than any of the other.

In addition William's birth of children, as well as William's later children, have put the other Windsors further of the royal throne.

It appears like over the years gatherings were restricted to family gatherings, like during Christmas and weddings.

Charles always loved Anne for her unassuming confidence however, she was also a bit snobbish toward his own quest for spiritual awakening.

When he was a teenager, Anne was heavily influenced by the work of the psychologist Sir Laurens van der Post. however to Anne his work, it was a 'mumbo mumbo'.

When Charles claimed he was cold from his parents' childhood, Anne refuted the claim totally.

She stated that her children were aware that the time they spent with her father and mother was not always easy however, within the family, life was as comfortable and as normal as it could be in the light of the scrutiny they were always subject to.

Charles His relationship with his younger twin brother Edward can at times have been fraught. For instance the time Edward was a participant in the film "It's A Royal Knockout' and when his TV company made use of his position by filming it in St Andrews.

It was also at a time when Prince William was starting his college life in the UK and an agreement was reached with the media to let Prince William to himself.

"He's an a**" Charles is believed to have said.

Perhaps it's the relationship between him and Andrew that makes him the most difficult. Charles was of the opinion that as he got in his teen years, Andrew got more of his mom's time than he did.

Furthermore, while Charles believed he was a serious thinker Andrew simply blinked at the privileges that came with his job.

The easy-going personality made his the life at Gordonstoun much more enjoyable to him than for his elder brother.

As he's gotten older, and assumed an increasingly important role in 'royal operation, Charles has pared down the size of his active family. This has led to, for his siblings and brothers having progressively less role in the family.

He offered Andrew an opportunity to work as an assistant, but it was rejected. Edward and Anne enjoy opening new structures and assisting charities.

However, the royal family as an institution of the public is now much more polished. It is a distinct lineage that runs from the Queen , Prince Philip through Charles and then down towards his sons.

At a younger age there was a closeness that is now more obvious as well as the affection shared between the parents and their son was not as evident.

From Charles from Charles' viewpoint. Charles was troubled by the bluntness of his father and mother's absence.

It's good to know that, as they get older and old at least to an outsider is stronger than it has ever been.

Poundbury, A Model Community

His Prince of Wales has believed in the rural landscape, urban development, along with architecture and landscapes as something that should be revered rather than being treated as a part of a centralised plan.

The town of Poundbury located in Dorset is his idea that has been brought to life. Ministers are often asked to join him on his trips, or go on a tour of the area to experience the village as it is.

In hopes that people could be inspired to adopt its principles as a policy for urban and environmental protection.

The village is currently under development. It was first inhabited in 1993. It is scheduled to be finished by 2025.

One of the main aspects of Poundbury is the significance it gives to people's lives over automobiles. The town aims to provide the traditional lifestyle, in which people's daily lives will be similar to that of their forefathers to generations.

The Prince was not the only visionary to establish their own community, to provide people with the kind of lifestyle they believe will be treasured.

Numerous magnates from the industrial age took the same route in building schools, housing, and often reaching the point of establishing guidelines for the lifestyle of what was usually the families of their workers.

Sons of the pioneer of chocolate John Cadbury, George and Richard developed the concept of Bourneville which is which is now located in Birmingham for their employees.

Their community was filled with every amenities, with only one exception: an establishment called a pub. Brothers were Quakers and were not a fan of drinking alcohol.

Cadbury employees were treated with respect and were paid a wage which was exceptional in the time. Their managers believed in the importance of being outdoors and created a space that encouraged swimming and walking.

As early as the turn of the century, residents of Bourneville even though they were mostly employed for the Cadbury plant were describing their neighborhood as one of the top locations to reside in Britain.

The Cadbury family was not the only ones to construct models of villages. Saltaire situated in West Yorkshire is another such area. It has recently achieved the status of being a UNESCO World Heritage Site.

Sir Titus Salt built the village in 1851. Similar villages, though smaller, were already effective in the area like Edward Akroyd's home in Copley.

Saltaire included a school, boathouse, allotments, Billiard room, concert hall and even a science lab.

Sir Titus was a champion of physical and mental health - his home had the gym and a reading area.

Furthermore, the tidy stone houses stood out against the slums of Bradford. He built bathing houses and put in the homes of his workers tap water.

Thus, Prince Charles is following the pattern of his predecessors with his project on Poundbury. When it is complete, the village will have residents of 6000 in 2500 houses.

Although it is commonly described as an area, Poundbury is actually simply part of the bigger city of Dorchester.

But, it's quite a distinct place. In contrast to how most cities and towns have grown through time There isn't any zoned area.

This is the method by which various parts of a city are assigned a specific function. For instance, one region could have large and expensive private residences. A different area could have smaller, private homes. A third of them could comprise of social housing. A different could be an industrial zone.

There are retail zones that are typically suburban or town centers.

However, Poundbury is not averse to this. In the Poundbury community, there may be found all of these components, they are mixed together. There is a detached five-bedroom house next to a small social housing area as well as the shops that are interspersed throughout the housing.

In reality, Poundbury is already playing part in the manner developments are growing. In either case the massive building projects being built around towns are a mixture of different types of housing.

The village's atmosphere the village, if you can be so kind is pleasant and practical. The houses are classic in design which means that even though it's not exactly modern, it still has the look of an older village.

The overall atmosphere is one of comfort and middle-class wealth. However the village is made up of over a third social housing. In the absence of a zone comprised of just these kinds of homes there is no sign of the ghettos that is often in these regions.

Prince Charles regards that the town as sanctuary for all. That is the impression that is felt by people who visit.

Furthermore the village has been operating as an enterprise commercial. It is not a mere scheme devised by an individual with influence , but no knowledge of reality The village is already contributing more than PS300 billion to its local economy and is expected to increase substantially when the village is fully operational.

Perhaps the Prince, more than being a meddling monarch an unpopular monarch, is someone who the politicians need to pay more attention.

Chapter 6: Diana

Though he may have known the details as he was in a relationship with Sarah Spencer, later Mccorquordale and Mccorquordale, there was a third member of the family who lit a huge candle in his honor.

This was the name of his potential future spouse, Diana.

They reconnected during the time that Charles played polo during an event. They quickly became friends and, soon Diana was invited to spend a week in the Royal Yacht Britannia.

After that, she went off to visit her parents in Balmoral.

"She's a member of our family, Queen Elizabeth declared of the girl. She was already aware of her, a boy who was a friend of Andrew and Edward while they were at Sandringham.

The Norfolk house didn't have an outdoor pool, however the Spencers who lived in a rented house on the estate didhave one, and the princes' younger brothers were able to take a dip in the pool along with a young Diana.

The media was extremely interested in Charles's love life and soon following the 1980 date it was clear to the press that something greater than his other relationships was forming.

The prince was surrounded by the protection that comes with being a royal and his access to him was restricted and restricted.

However, this was not the case for his partner, and she was the target of incessant interference.

The situation deteriorated so dire that Queen Elizabeth II herself attempted to intervene in the matter, contacting editors to convince the journalists to take their photographers and photographers.

The move didn't work for long, and it was not a big achievement.

Charles and Diana began their relationship on February 1, 1981. just one month into their marriage.

Even at this point doubts were running through his head. The only genuine deep, romantic love in his life and she was not available to a potential heir. Of course, about Camilla.

While playing the game and clearly expressing his feelings, Charles said in interviews following the wedding that he felt "delighted and genuinely amazed that Diana is willing to be my partner.'

Most famously, there's an embarrassingly awkward interview with Andrew Carthew, a journalist associated with ITN.

A man asks his couple whether they're in love. This is a question that appears to be, for a newly-engaged couple, to be a bit odd.

Maybe the interviewer had something that the public did not.

Diana replies in a manner that is largely convincing "Of course.'

Charles's response is, but, it's not as positive. "Whatever "in love" means",' he states. The smile his wife's face, looking back tells us that this isn't an ideal marriage.

The couple got married on the 29th of July, 1981. The world went crazy. It was a wedding 'made out of heaven'.

In fact, it was like a fairytale. The charming young prince wearing a medal-adorned uniform, had his destiny as the king was planned.

And his innocent, young gorgeous, charming and coy bride. We now realize that things were not exactly heavenly.

On the day of the wedding, such was his displeasure at getting married to an individual who appeared to have affection, but not total love, that he told his aide "I'm not going to do the wedding.'

He was aware that, beneath her appearance, his wife was a woman suffering. She was already suffering from the pain that comes with an eating disorder. She was a vulnerable and complex.

It wasn't something with that Charles was experienced. The life experiences of a prince were scarce.

While she was at it, Diana knew that her husband had close to Camilla. She found a bracelet for his partner, which was that was engraved in G and F. This may have been referring to their nicknames for to each other, Gladys as well as Fred.

The wedding did take place, and according to the instructions she received that they were not able to quit because their faces were already on tea towels.'

For Charles his country girl was actually a complicated woman, with many anxieties. For Diana her husband, he loved an additional woman and always did.

In reality, Diana and Camilla were extremely close, the elder woman sometimes serving as a confidant to the young, soon to be princess.

Diana was pregnant and suffered a lot through the pregnancy process. However, Charles was of the most the traditional lineage as it's likely to happen.

His father was one who believed that to be sick was a sign of weakness and Diana would just have to live with her condition and move back to living.

Charles was at times, he later admitted in the end, out of his element.

Things changed following William's birth. William. However, it was only for a short time. While his affair with Camilla was in full swing, Diana was involved in her own affairs.

After she was pregnant for another time Charles did his best to be aware of the various conditions associated with pregnancy. And when she was ill again He was extremely supportive.

Following Harry's birth appeared good for a time. But then the pattern resurfaced and relationships outside of the marriage still thriving for both.

In public, at times the icy gulf between them was glaringly apparent.

The Prince was raised to be a man of service, Diana wished to be a mother. The princess wanted her kids to be close to her. They would soon be enrolled at the Prep School close to London and she would frequently be there to watch school games.

The two became more and more discordant. A heated argument broke out. Charles seeking to go shooting with his sons but Diana was keen to keep them the house with her.

"She's mad, mad insane!' He is reported to have yelled to his mother.

With the press always eager to share real or false tales of their marriage failing The Queen decided to keep the issue off.

Aided by a colleague, she explained that she had been taught how to handle problems of the country by making things into compartments, and this was the reason why the door into the compartment to be securely locked.

However, their marriage would be resuscitated, and it fell to the then Prime Minister at the moment, John Major, to publicly announce their separation. separated.

The Queen reacted seriously. Media and the public however, were divided on their beliefs. One side was a family that was bound by privilege, tradition and the veil. On the other hand, the beautiful young mother who placed her children first and the rest of her family first.

The idea of a ruling class was new to her.

It's no surprise that Diana was a constant symbol of love. Charles and the rest of the family which included Charles were viewed as an unconnected family that had no relationship to reality.

And obviously, Diana was a delightful person. Someone with a clear and evident sense of kindness and a smoky smile, and someone who believed in the weak.

Charles on the contrary, was trained to be rigid and formal in a way that was that was inaccessible.

Diana is Diana, Charles was Sir. There were some who appreciated the formality however, they were the majority.

The couple split in 1996. At that point, Diana was approaching a status that was close to sainthood in the eyes the general public.

Her affair was forgiven as a result of a young woman being trapped in a marriage that was not a loving one to cold in-laws and an unfaithful husband.

Her work with victims of aids proved her to be one of one of the most knowledgeable of all. She was, and it wasn't just a facade. Her sons were loved and she was seen as the responsible parent.

The conflicting opinions intensified by the media who were content to portray Charles as the villain in any controversy. However the invasive interferences in her private life by paparazzi also won her the attention of the public.

However, where there is an actress, there must be an antagonist.

The situation could not be better for the prince. So he thought. After his ex-wife was killed in a vehicle crash, his life was at low.

The stories already circulated about the palace's attempts to invade Diana's house. Her remarks about "dark forces' working could be interpreted as that the people who work for Windsor's House of Windsor.

Theorists of conspiracy theories quickly claim the theory that Prince Phillip was behind the murder of his son - and that it was an assassination and not an accident.

If Charles as well as his family stayed William and Harry away from the limelight immediately following her death, it wasn't regarded as caretaking acts of fathers or grandparents.

While some people could see the logic however, many people did not. It was because of Diana's status to the general public that she was considered to be the queen of the people which meant that her sons were considered to be the nation's princes.

They were looking for comfort and to be a comfort to them. Of course, looking back we can see the resemblance of care and concern towards William Harry and William. Harry.

They are two boys whose mother sudden and unintentionally passed away. The boys later found out that they had talked to her in the evening and were both in a hurry to call in the hope of returning to their other pursuits.

What feeling of guilt must they have experienced. How much sorrow and desperation. Not only was an awful death yet the mourning will be much more visible than one could ever imagine.

Of course, they'd prefer to enjoy the safety of their families. Of course, they'd like for their the only remaining parent.

But , the public was not keen to believe that at the time.

After the ceremony, which was, according to some, an issue that was influenced by politics for the government of the Labour Party that was in place at the time Charles' and the royal family's respect in the eyes of the public fell to the lowest point of all time.

A Father Loving

If Charles as he grew older, decided to see a modernization of the monarchy, then it is the role his sons have adopted.

We can see in them a desire to share their views with the general public, to comment in the cause of their mother but also as they grew older and determined to be young men.

One of the reasons Phillip was insistent that Charles should go to Gordonstoun rather than Eton was the belief that Eton would be a target for harassment by the media.

However, Charles and Diana made sure that this did never happen to boys in their school or their university days.

William is currently trying to do the same for William's own kids. The British media has expressed frustration with foreign paparazzi who have broken the rules that they are required to be adhering.

But, it was their decision to adhered to their own positions.

It is a huge merit to the Prince that he was able to appreciate the importance of fatherhood.

Perhaps he was not the image of the Queen or Prince Philip when they were put to serve on multiple occasions. Yet it appears that he always made sure that his sons were first.

When they are in their 30s look like mature intelligent, thoughtful, and well-intentioned men. They seem to be as connected with the world as those with this level of privilege could be.

But, if you look at their early years, this could seem like a surprise. How many of them are able to watch their parents going through a bitter divorce? Are they able to see it unfold in the public space?

Will they be able to cope with the sudden loss of their mother, and develop into excellent young men? Their mother's love gave them the foundations for this, and the rest is due to their father.

Princess Diana and Prince Phillip as well have been very supportive of their grandson. Particularly when it comes to looking after their children and keeping them away from the spotlight of attention following the death of their mother.

I'm sure we'll never be able to determine the truth however it is thought that exposing the children to the public by letting them walk behind the coffin in the funeral of their mother was political instigated.

Whatever good-hearted the public may be, it's impossible to not imagine some anger from the young boys who felt that their private grievances were being relegated to the general public.

Harry was hesitant to go out, and who would blame him. The reason is Prince Philip who convinced Harry. "If I leave, can you be with me?' he asked.

Charles himself was a man who treated his children as adults at an young age. He believed in explaining and reason, not discipline.

Although he was in a way a man who was educated against emotional displays in public He was still charming and loving in private.

People close to his family say that the time he had with his children was of the finest quality.

They would travel to Gloucestershire on weekends, and then when Charles arrived, typically later after an official event, they would race into his helicopter to greet Charles, frequently jumping onto his shoulders.

In the months after Diana's death The Queen wanted to have him open his relationship to Camilla more open, but he remained adamant to keep his sons safe from further public scrutiny.

He had spoken about his relationship shortly before her death, however William particularly was not keen to talk about the matter.

The matter was not discussed until the older son wanted to see her later. However, even then, the boys were allowed to set the pace at which they would get to know their stepmom.

There is a tale of Charles taking a young William to his farm as a pre-schooler. The weather is cold and the boy starts to complain about his hands hurting.

I told you to wear gloves, but you didn't. Also you should stop complaining. You could imagine an infant Charles being scolded by his father many years prior to.

You are the parent, at least in the beginning days, the same way you the parent you were. Charles however has changed and has mellowed. The real character of Charles has been revealed.

If the story were to be re-created today , with Charles and his children It is possible to imagine that his gloves will be in his purse and he will be putting them on with great care.

He has a close relationship William as well as Harry is loving and warm. As Philip has to his grandkids it is easy to imagine Charles enjoying his own children.

Camilla At Last

Extra marital relations within the monarchy aren't an original idea. In the time in the reign of Edward VII, the king had one or two wives.

One of them were Alice Keppel; she happened to be the great great-grandmother of the individual who was, according to Diana who was her bride, caused her wedding to be somewhat too crowded.

"There were always three of us within this wedding', she once stated.

We are discussing Camilla.

Prince Charles was introduced to Camilla Shand during an event in polo in 1970. They instantly fell in love with each other and started an affair.

However, the Princely tradition must be adhered to and, when the new Prince of the throne joined the navy his assignments led to a conflict in the relationship and eventually it came to an end.

In the past time, Princess Ann was in love with an earlier boyfriend. This man named Andrew Parker Bowles. Andrew Parker Bowles.

If the story were to be told in fiction, the majority of people would consider the plot is too unbelievable. It is however factual that the great-great granddaughter of a previous royal mistress and the an ex-girlfriend of the future king's wife married the man who had been dating the heir's daughter. More bizarre twists and turns will come!

In the other hand the circles within which royals move were, prior to the 1970s, and even before the 1970s, rather tiny.

Camilla Andrew and Camilla Andrew were blessed with two kids. Tom was born a year later than the wedding in 1974 was Prince Charles' godson.

Ummm. Godfather and Stepfather This is an unorthodox combination. But, it would have to wait for a long time.

A second daughter was born, in 1978. Laura. Laura's daughter was an attendant at a important royal wedding.

The wedding of Prince William to Kate Middleton.

While both were married, it appears that Camilla and Charles remain extremely close throughout.

In addition, it was a lot worse beginning in 1986. Charles and Diana's relationship was already deteriorating The same was applicable to Camilla's. While she didn't meet her stepsons for another 12 years the couple Charles enjoyed a lot of time together.

The year 2003 was the time that Camilla relocated to Clarence House, Charles' official residence. Their engagement was publicized in 2005 and they got married in the following year.

It was a peaceful private affair. Prince William was the best man and only a few guests were present. The guests, which are worth noting that Andrew Parker Bowles and his second wife.

The Queen was, during the period following Diana's death, worried about her relationship between the two. On one other hand, she wanted his son content.

On the other hand, the reputation and name associated with Windsor's House of Windsor was, and remains, of paramount important to Her.

Around the turn into the twentieth century Charles his relationship to Camilla was a private affair. Camilla was worried about the possibility that Charles might end up as a King with a woman in love which could harm the monarchy.

Additionally, she was afraid of an outcry from the public if couple got married too early after her death. Diana. At the time, it was the time when the Royal family seemed to be in the lowest point in the eyes of the public.

It was considered to be the villain as the villain, with Charles as the principal character in the tragic event that eventually led to the people's"Princess's" death.

The Queen was stunned and dismayed when she first discovered, years earlier the affair of her son with a woman who was married.

In actual fact, Camilla had been banned from the palace grounds and frequently removed from guest lists that she could have expected to appear on.

There was more intrigue in the complicated web of connections. Andrew Parker Bowles was the godson of the Queen Mother.

What an awful mess!

The Queen had been friends with Camilla for a number of years and she was a bit disappointed by the friendship, as well as the secrecy that surrounded it.

A equerry remembered 'I remember Andrew and Camilla staying with us. The equerry went on to add that the Queen was acquainted with Camilla "for all time" as well as that the two were great friends.

What was going on in the background was something which she was unable to approve.

Maybe, in the end, it was Camilla whom was blamed by the Queen for the scandal. She was an adultererous lady who misled her son.

The majority of mothers, in the same situation, will likely consider that way.

The Queen then began to think differently. Evidently, she was cleaning the cabinet of candles on Balmoral when the thought struck her.

The relationship needed to be more transparent. In the end the Queen let Camilla to return to her the official world.

Her first appearance was at a dinner for a group of wealthy Americans who had donated to the Prince's charitable causes.

He gave a speech and included a line which was not well-received when his mother was informed of the speech.

She wasn't present at this particular dinner and the son of her said:

When the cat is gone, the mice play.'

However, to the Queen, things were just too serious to be jokes. Camilla was in the minds of the Diana loving people, number one public enemy.

She was aware that not just was she getting older in her years, but also the possibility of an incident or attack had always been there. 'Uncle Dickie' Mountbatten had been murdered. She herself had come across an uninvited visitor in her bedroom.

Shots (they proved to be blanks, however she didn't know it) were fired while she was riding their horse Burmese in the Horse Guards' Parade.

What would the people of the nation think when her son became King with a girlfriend? This was not something that anyone should think about.

However her son was clearly in love with Camilla and she was enthralled with her. He had declared that the relationship was 'non-negotiable.'

The days that he been threatening to kill his butler Paul Burrell, for giving an indication Diana Diana that he could be in the wrong long gone.

The Queen's private secretary Sir Robert Fellowes, had gone to the extent of telling the Prince to abdicate Camilla in order to preserve the monarchy.

He was told the straight refusal. It was a great thing for Prince Charles. It was that distant and gloomy presentation of the monarchy that seemed way out of date.

Had he opted in the past to let go of his personal desires for a general sense of duty to the public The monarchy today probably wouldn't be in the strong and well-liked position it is in today.

The times change, people change however, some of the old guards can are slower to catch up.

Her suggestion to the queen was Camilla was to be "official" during weekends only.

She was not present at the civil ceremony that was held at the wedding, but she joined the couple in a private ceremony during the ceremony at Windsor Castle, then hosted an extravagant reception.

In the course of this, she delivered an address that for a horse-loving woman such as the Queen was a sign of her love for her son and desire to ensure his happiness were the top priorities.

She told them that they had beaten Becher's Brook and The Chair (two of the most difficult fences in the Grand National). She was also proud that of them for having done it.

Today, the bond between them is friendly and warm. They are frequently seen in public, sharing laughter and jokes.

The union between Charles as well as Camilla is solid and stable.

Chapter 7: Awareness Of The Natural Environment

Charles has been a proponent of environmental awareness in the late 1970s. In his role as the chair of the Welsh Countryside Committee, he gave his first public address on environmental issues at 21. To cut down on the carbon footprint of his business, he's used biomass boilers to heat Birkhall which is where he built a hydroelectric generator at the property's river. Additionally, he has set up solar panels on Clarence House and Highgrove, is driving the Aston Martin DB6 on E85 and has electric vehicles at his estates. Charles is an avid gardening enthusiast, also emphasized the importance of talking to and listening to plants noting "I am a happy person to talk with as well as listen to trees and plants. I believe that it is essential."

After the move to Highgrove House, Charles developed an desire to grow organically, which led him to launch of his organic company, Duchy Originals, in 1990. Duchy Originals now sells more than 200 products that are sustainably made that range from food to garden furniture. The earnings (over PS6 million in 2010) go towards the Prince's Charities. Charles was co-author (with Charles Clover and environment editor of The Daily Telegraph) Highgrove: A Comprehensive Experiment in Organic Gardening and Farming that was which was published in 1993 to record the activities on his property and is also patronized by Garden Organic. Similar to this, Charles became interested in agriculture and the various industries it supports and regularly visited farmers to discuss their business. Despite the foot-and-mouth disease of 2001 in England was a deterrent to Charles from exploring the organic fields of

Saskatchewan and farms, he did meet the farmer at Assiniboia town hall. Mutton Renaissance Campaign Mutton Renaissance Campaign, which was launched in 2004 was designed to help promote British producers of sheep and to help make mutton more appealing to Britons. Media have been critical of his organic farmingpractices: According the The Independent on October 2006, "the story of Duchy Originals has seen some ethical issues and compromises coupled with a fervent marketing program." A vocal advocate of the practice He has been vocal about the use of the genetically altered (GM) crops and also criticized the creation of food products that have been genetically modified in a 1998 letter addressed to Tony Blair. He reaffirmed the same views, saying that "one kind of amazing technological advancement after another... is going to lead to the biggest environmental disaster ever recorded."

He won the 10th Global Environmental Citizen Award (GECA) from Harvard Medical School's Center for Health and the Environment Director, Eric Chivian, said: "For decades, the Prince of Wales has been an outstanding advocate for nature. He has been a renowned leader in the fight to increase efficiency in energy use and lessen toxic substances' release into the air, land as well as the oceans." "Plane Stupid's Joss Garman was critical of Charles's personal plane usage for travel. In 2007 Charles founded his organization, the Prince's May Day Network, an organization which encourages businesses to act against climate change. In February of 2008 Charles spoke to his fellow members of the European Parliament and urged European Union leaders to combat massive environmental change. The audience applauded him. Nigel Farage, the United Kingdom Independence Party leader was seated and said that Charles's advisers were "Quiet ignorant and stupid at the very best." In his speech in participants at the Low Carbon Prosperity Summit in the European Parliament on the 9th of February 2011 Charles declared that climate change deniers are playing "a risky gamble" in their beliefs about the Future of the planet and have an "corrosive influence" on the public's opinions. In addition, he stressed the importance of safeguarding fisheries and the Amazon rainforest in addition to making low carbon emissions more accessible and competitive. Charles was awarded the Royal Society for the Protection of Birds Medal in 2011 for his environmental work which included the protection of forests.

Charles addressed the audience on July 27, 2012 during the International Union for Conservation of Nature at the World Conservation Congress in support of the belief that animals that graze are essential to keep healthy grasslands and soils:

I've been fascinated at the efforts of a remarkable man called Allan Savory in Zimbabwe and other semi-arid areas, who have been arguing for years against the conventional wisdom that the simple presence of cattle leads to desertification and overgrazing. Contrarily the way he has shown in a way that is clear, the land needs the presence of feed animals and their droppings in order to complete the cycle, ensuring that grassland areas and soils remain productive. So the land will end up dying when you eliminate grazers from the fields and place them in huge feedlots.

The month of February was when Prince Charles visited Somerset to visit residents who had been affected by winter flooding. In his trip, Prince Charles stated, "There's nothing like a good catastrophe to inspire people to take action. It's tragic that nothing has was done for such a long time." He made a PS50,000 contribution of the Prince's Countryside Fund to assist families and companies. In December 2015, Charles delivered a statement at the opening ceremony of COP21, urging the industry to cease deforestation-causing practices. In August of 2019 the media revealed that Prince Charles collaborated together with British Fashion designers Vin Omi and Vin Omi to design a line of clothing made from nettles that were that were found at the estate of his Highgrove estate. Nettles are a species of plant that is typically "seen as useless." The plant's residues taken from Highgrove were also used for the creation of jewelry alongside the clothing. In September of 2020, Charles established RE: TV the first online platform featuring short films, as well as writings about sustainability and climate change subjects. Charles serves as the site's chief editor. The site later teamed to Amazon Prime Video and WaterBear another streaming service that is devoted to environmental issues. The same month, the president suggested during a talk that fighting climate change needs an international response that is comparable as Marshall Plan. Marshall Plan.

Charles presented Charles introduced the Sustainable Markets Initiative during the annual gathering at Charles at the World Economic Forum in Davos, Switzerland, in January 2020. The initiative aims to put sustainability at the heart of all initiatives. It was in the month of May that Charles Sustainable Markets Initiative and the (WEF) World Economic Forum introduced The Great Reset project, a five-point plan that aims to foster sustainable economic growth following the aftermath of

COVID-19's global depression. On January 20, 2021 Charles announced Terra Carta ("Earth Charter") which is the first sustainable financial charter, which requires members to comply with standards in order to make their business more sustainable. They also invest in causes and projects that help protect the environment. In July 2021 Charles as well as Jony Ive unveiled that they would launch the Terra Carta Design Lab, which was a contest launched in collaboration with the Royal College of Art to discover solutions to environmental and climate problems. The winners would receive financial assistance and would be presented to the Sustainable Markets Initiative's top industry experts. Then, in September of 2021 Charles launched Food for the Future, an initiative with the help of Jimmy Doherty and Jamie Oliver that seeks to teach secondary school children regarding the system of eating and to eliminate food waste. As a great supporter of the National Hedgelaying Society, Charles has hosted receptions for the competition's rural component on his Highgrove estate in order to conserve hedgerows that were planted within The United Kingdom.

He was a guest at an official banquet hosted by Queen Elizabeth at the 47th G7 summit and also an exchange of ideas with G7 leaders and CEOs from sustainable industries, to look at ways to solve corporate and government environmental challenges. In his address during the 2021 G20 gathering in Rome in June, he described COP26 as "the last saloon" to combat climate change , and demanded that efforts be undertaken to bring about a green-friendly sustainable and environmentally sustainable economy. In his speech at the the opening ceremony of COP26 in Rome, he reiterated his ideas from last year, saying that "a huge military-style effort" was needed "to mobilise the forces of the global business community" to tackle climate change. In the summer of 2021 Prince Charles addressed the BBC on the topic of the environment, and said that he doesn't eat fish nor meat for every two days and consumes dairy products once a week.

The Climate Action Scholarships for a variety of student groups from island countries were launched in the month of the month of March in 2022, by Charles as director of the Cambridge Institute for Sustainability Leadership and in collaboration together with Universities of Cambridge, Toronto, Melbourne, McMaster, and Montreal. In September of 2022 Charles was the host of his first Global Allergy Symposium at Dumfries House together with The Natasha Allergy Research Foundation and 16 allergy experts from all over the globe who came together to examine and discuss the aspects that lead to the rise of new allergies.

Interest in alternative medicine

Charles has been criticized for his support of alternative medicine. In a lecture in December 1982 at members of the British Medical Association, he made his first public statement of interest in alternative medical practices. Medical and scientific experts were opposed to the Prince's Foundation of Integrated Health's (FIH) campaign that urged general practitioners to provide alternatives to conventional treatments and herbal remedies for National Health Service patients. In a speech to healthcare professionals at a meeting on the 24th of June 2004, he advocated the use of Gerson therapies like coffee enemas for treating cancer patients with terminal illness and said he had a connection to one of these patients. These comments were criticized by medical experts , such that of Michael Baum. In a speech in May 2006 before the World Health Assembly in Geneva, Charles called for merging conventional and alternative medical practices and advocated for the use of homeopathy.

The month of April, 2008 The Times published a special letter from Edzard Ernst who is professor of Complementary Medicine at the University of Exeter, requesting that the FIH take down two guides that promote alternative medicine due to the fact that "the vast majority of these alternative treatments appear to be ineffective clinically and a lot of them are risky." A representative from the FIH has responded to the criticism by saying: "We categorically refute the assertion that our website publication Complementary Healthcare Complementary Healthcare: A Comprehensive Guide is a source of any false or misleading information about the benefits of alternative treatments. It, however, views people as adults and takes the responsible approach by insisting that they consult reliable sources of information so that they can make informed decisions. The foundation doesn't support alternative therapies." In the year 2000, Ernst co-authored a book along with Simon Singh entitled Trick or Treatment The alternative Medicine on Trial. It was humorously dedicated to "HRH the Prince of Wales."

Edzard Ernst was adamant about the "Detox Tincture" developed through Charles's Duchy Originals as "financially abusing the weak" and "complete fraud." In 2009 the Advertising Standards Authority condemned an email that was sent out from Duchy Originals to advertise their Echina-Relief Hyperi-Lift and Detox Tinctures as misleading. Charles sent seven letters addressed to Medicines and Healthcare products Regulatory Agency (MHRA) prior to the time they changed the rules governing the labeling of these herbal remedies. Medical and scientific organizations have been vocally scathing about this decision. Then, in October of 2009 the media reported in the press that Prince Charles had personally urged Health Secretary Andy Burnham for the NHS to expand its options for alternatives to treatments.

In April 2010, as a result of accounting concerns An ex-FIH official as well as his wife were arrested under suspicion of PS300,000 fraud. The next day the FIH announced the end of its operations and stated that "its principal goal of promoting the utilization in integrated healthcare" was met. George Gray, the charity's accounting director and finance director, was found guilty and sentenced three years in prison for the theft of PS253,000. The FIH was changed and relaunched as The College of Medicine in the year 2010. Charles was named a patron of the foundation in the year the year 2019. In the year 2016, Charles stated in a speech that he was reducing usage of antibiotics in his farm through remedies for veterinary medicine that are homeopathic. On June 27, 2019 Charles was named patron of the Faculty of Homeopathy, drawing controversy.

Chapter 8: Philosophy And Religion.

Concerns

Charles was formally confirmed at the age of 16 by Archbishop Canterbury Michael Ramsey in St George's Chapel in Windsor Castle during Easter 1965. While in Balmoral Castle, Charles attends the Church of Scotland's Crathie Kirk along with the other members in the Royal Family. In addition, he attends various Anglican churches located close to Highgrove. He was in 2000 when he received the title of the Lord High Commissar to Scotland's Church's General Assembly. Charles has been to in a manner that was largely secretive, Eastern Orthodox monasteries on Mount Athos in Romania and Serbia at numerous times. Charles is also patron to the Oxford Centre for Islamic Studies at the University of Oxford. He was the founder of the Markfield Institute of Higher Education in the twenty-first century. It is dedicated to Islamic studies within a multi-cultural and pluralistic context.

Sir Laurens van der Post became Charles's friend in 1977. He was referred to as his "spiritual Guru" as well as Prince William's godfather. Charles was introduced to the philosophy of mind and a fascination with different religious traditions from van der Post. Charles shared his philosophical thoughts in his Nautilus Book Award winning book, Harmony: A New Way of Viewing Our World. In November of 2016 the Prince was present at the dedication of the very first Syriac Orthodox cathedral in Britain, St Thomas Cathedral in Acton. In October of 2019 He was a guest at Cardinal Newman's canonization. On January 20, 2020 Charles was in contact with representatives of the Eastern

Churches at Jerusalem. The meeting concluded with an interfaith celebration in Bethlehem's Church of the Nativity in Bethlehem Then, Christian as well as Muslim leaders led Charles on a trip around the city.

Despite speculation that Charles promised to remain "Defender of faiths" as well as "Defender of Faith" as the King, he declared in 2015 that he will continue to hold the monarch's title that reads "Defender of the Faith" as well as "making sure that the other beliefs can be followed," which he sees as the duty to the Church of England.

Pre-accession polling

Before he was crowned the British throne, polls put Charles's popularity among British population at 42%. This was based on an 18-month BMG Research survey revealing that 46 percent of Britons were in favor of

Charles to abdicate as soon as he was his accession to the throne to be replaced by William. Sixty percent of British people had a favorable view of Charles according to an opinion poll conducted in 2021.

Plans for coronation and accession

Charles was crowned his place on the British throne on the 8th of September 2022, following the death of his mother queen, Elizabeth II, died. Charles was the longest-serving British succession heir in April 20th, 2011 surpassing the record of Edward VII. When he was crowned King at the age of 73 He was the oldest person to achieve this over William IV, who was just 64 when he was crowned the Great King in 1830.

Charles' coronation Charles is scheduled with the help of code name Operation Golden Orb. Edward Fitzalan-Howard, the 18th Duke of Norfolk who is still a holder of the title of hereditary Earl Marshal, is the chairman of the committee. The committee is composed of notable Aristocratic members and other dignitaries, this committee is legally distinct from the office that are held by Charles III or the Queen. According to some reports Charles' coronation could be less complicated and smaller in magnitude than the coronation of his mother in 1953.

There were rumors about the title that the regnal Charles could choose to take upon taking the throne. In 2005 there was a report that Charles was King. Charles had suggested that he could decide to rule as George VII in honor of his maternal grandfather and keep away from the Stuart King Charles I and Charles I, who were executed, and Charles II, who was beheaded. Charles II, who was famous for his raunchy lifestyle and was aware of the great legacy of Bonnie Prince Charlie, a Stuart contender of his father's English as well as Scottish thrones, who was referred to by the name of "Charles III" by his supporters. As of 2005, the government of Charles said that no decision was taken. Clarence House confirmed that King Charles will use the royal designation "Charles III" after the demise of queen Elizabeth II.

Charles gave his inaugural speech to the nation on September 9 at 18:00 BST In it, Charles lamented the loss his mother, and christened William Prince of Wales as his child. William Prince of Wales.

On the 10th of September 2022, 2022 on September 10, 2022, the Accession Council openly proclaimed Charles as King. The ceremony was first shown on TV. William Prince of Wales as well as the Queen Camilla were among those who attended as were former British premier Ministers Sir John Major, Tony Blair, Gordon Brown, David Cameron Lady (Theresa) May along with Boris Johnson.

Marriages and relations

Bachelorhood

In his early years, Charles had romantic relationships with several women. His great-uncle Lord Mountbatten who advised Charles at the moment: In a circumstance similar to yours, a man should plant his delicious wild oats and go through as many relationships as he can before making a decision to a woman to be a life partner it is best to choose a compatible attractive, beautiful, and sweet girl before she has had a chance to meet anyone else she could find love with. When a woman marries, if they have to be in a position of honor this can be a traumatic experience for them to experience.

Georgiana Russell, the daughter of the British ambassador to Spain Sir John Russell; Lady Jane Wellesley the gorgeous child of the eight Duke of Wellington; Davina Sheffield; Lady Sarah Spencer; and Camilla Shand, who was later his second wife were among Charles his close friends.

In the spring of 1974 Mountbatten was in contact with Charles regarding a potential wedding to Mountbatten's daughter Amanda Knatchbull. Charles sent an email to the mother of Amanda's Lady Brabourne who was his godmother, to express his desire to marry her daughter. Lady Brabourne was a positive response, but she pointed out that a romantic interest of the girl wasn't quite 17 yet, seemed too young. Mountbatten made plans for Amanda as well as himself to accompany Charles in his tour in India four years afterward. Philip thought that Charles was going to be ostracized from his famed Uncle and Lord Brabourne recommended that a trip to India in tandem could draw the attention of the cousins, before they could choose whether to wed.

Mountbatten was murdered in the hands of his fellow soldiers of the Irish Republican Army in August 1979, prior to his departure by Prince Charles on his own to India. After his return to England, he made a proposal to Amanda who was wary of joining the royal family following the loss of her paternal grandmother, grandfather and younger brother Nicholas during the attack. In June of 1980, Charles formally declined Chevening House which was open to him since 1974, to be his next home. Chevening was a home that was once a landmark located in Kent was given to the Crown and was also an endowment given by the final Earl Stanhope, Amanda's childless great-uncle with the intention that Charles would eventually reside there. The year 1977 was the first time a paper mistakenly stated that Charles got engaged to princess Marie-Astrid, a native of Luxembourg.

Marriages

Wedding to Lady Diana Spencer

Charles was introduced to the beautiful Lady Diana Spencer for the first time in 1977, when the two visited her house, Althorp. Sarah was his partner, and he didn't consider Diana romantically until around the middle of the 1980s. In July, as Charles and Diana were sitting on a haybale at an event hosted by a friend, Diana noticed that he appeared depressed and needed care in the wake of the great uncle Lord Mountbatten. She was with him on his visits to Balmoral Castle and Sandringham House. According to his biographer, Jonathan Dimbleby, "without an obvious display of emotional emotion" Charles began to consider her a possible wedding bride. She also was with him on these trips.

Charles his uncle Norton Knatchbull and his wife reported that Diana was amazed by his height and Charles didn't seem as if he was in love. In the meantime, the media and photographers were attentive to the ongoing romance between the couple. Charles saw his father's words as a warning to move forward immediately, when Prince Philip advised him that Diana's reputation could be damaged if he chose to not make a decision to marry her in the near future. After recognizing that Diana was in line with Mountbatten's requirements for the perfect royal bride Charles was able to interpret his father's words as a direction to take action immediately.

Charles offered to marry Lady Diana in February 1981. she agreed, and on the 29th of July 1981, they got wedding at St. Paul's Cathedral. Charles reduced his tax-free contribution from the income from his father's Duchy of Cornwall to 50 percent to 25% following his wedding. The couple lived on the grounds of Kensington Palace and Highgrove House near Tetbury with two kids: Prince William (born around 1982) as well as Prince Henry ("Harry") (b. 1984). Charles set a precedent in the history of royal births by becoming the first royal father to be present at to the child's births.

The marriage was in danger within five years due their incompatibility as well as a 13 years of age gap. Charles started his relationship to Camilla Parker Bowles in the month of November 1986. Diana confessed in a documentary released in 1992 produced by Peter Settelen that by

1986 she was "seriously in love with a person who was working in this particular environment." The story goes that Diana had been talking to Barry Mannakee, who was transferred into the Diplomatic Protection Squad in 1986 after his management found his interactions with Diana insensitive. Then, Diana began a connection with her family's former riding instructor Major James Hewitt. Charles and Diana's apparent displeasure at each other's presence led to tabloids naming the pair "The Gangsters." Diana revealed Charles' affair together with Camilla within the novel Diana, Her True Story by Andrew Morton.

In addition, audio recordings of her sexually explicit affairs have surfaced. There is a persistent belief of Hewitt has been Prince Harry's father have been basing in Hewitt as well as Harry's physical likeness. But, Harry was already born prior to the time Diana and Hewitt's relationship began.

Divorce and separation

In December 1992 the Premier John Major informed Parliament of the couple's legal separation. In the previous year was when the British press had published the recordings of a passionate phone conversation in 1989 with Prince Charles and Camilla, affectionately known as Camillagate. Charles III sought to gain public acceptance in a TV documentary titled Charles the Private Man and the public Role and with narration by Jonathan Dimbleby and aired on June 29th in 1994. In an interview within the movie, Charles discussed his extramarital relationship with Camilla who claimed that he had rekindled their romance in 1986, only when his union with Diana had ended in a tragic way. Then Diana made an admission of marital problems during an interview on BBC present

affairs show Panorama that was broadcast on November 20, 1995. She commented on Charles's relationship to Camilla, "Well, there were three of us at the royal wedding which made it quite packed." She also expressed doubt about Charles's ability to succeed to the throne. Charles and Diana split on the 28th of August of 1996, following an official instructions from the Queen to end their union in December 1995. Diana was killed by a car crash at Paris the 31st of August, 1997. Charles and Diana's daughters travelled to Paris to take Diana's corpse on her way back Britain.

Royal wedding ceremony with Camilla Parker Bowles

Charles and Camilla Parker's wedding took place on Feb. 10, 2005 and he also presented her with an engagement ring that was a gift from his maternal grandmother. According to the Royal Marriages Act of 1772 The Queen's approval to the wedding was confirmed at the Privy Council meeting on March 2. In the same meeting, Canadian Department of Justice declared that Queen's Privy Council for Canada was not required to convene to sign a consent form to the marriage because the union wouldn't result in children and not affect the succession of the Canadian throne.

Charles is the sole member in his British Royal family who chose to hold the option of a civil wedding in addition to a traditional church wedding. The BBC published administration records dating from 1950 and the 1960s, suggesting that such a wedding was illegal. Charles's spokesman denied the documents, and the current government clarified that they were outdated.

The civil ceremony was scheduled to take place on Windsor Castle, followed by the blessing of the church during the ceremony at St. George's Chapel. Since a civil wedding at Windsor Castle would require the location to be open for anyone wanting to marry there, the location was changed in the direction of Windsor Guildhall. In order to allow Charles as well as other invited guests to attend to his funeral for John Paul II, Pope John Paul II, the wedding was moved back from the initial day of April 8 until the next day, four days prior to the wedding.

The Queen's hesitation to be at the wedding could be due to her position as the Chief Governor for the Church of England. Charles' parents didn't attend the ceremony of civil marriage. The Duke and the Queen of Edinburgh were present for the blessing ceremony and then held the gathering held at Windsor Castle for the newlyweds. The blessing ceremony conducted by Rowan Williams, Archbishop of Canterbury on the steps of St. George's Chapel, Windsor Castle, was broadcast on television.

Personal passions

Sports

From his early years up to in 1992 Charles played competitive Polo player. In his death in 2005, he was able play informally, even for charitable causes. He had two surgeries to fix broken bones in his right arm. The injuries were sustained in a few instances when he fell off horses. Charles was a fox hunter frequently from the time of 2005 at which point the practice was banned across the United Kingdom. People who opposed the practice believed Charles's participation as an "political assertion" during the latter part of the 1990s as opposition towards the sport increased. In 1999 The League Against Cruel Sports launched an attack on Charles for taking his children into hunts like the Beaufort Hunt. The government was trying to stop hunting by hounds. He broke a bones in the left side of his shoulder while hunter within Derbyshire at the time in.

Since the age of his youth, Charles has been an avid salmon fisherman and has backed Orri Vigfsson's efforts to protect North Atlantic salmon. Charles usually fishes on in the River Dee in Aberdeenshire, Scotland however, one of his most memorable fishing experiences took place during his time in Vopnafjordur, Iceland. Charles is an avid Burnley Football Club supporter.

Visual, performing and new arts

Charles is the patron or president of over twenty organizations that perform arts that include The Royal College of singing, the Royal Opera, the English Chamber Orchestra as well as the Philharmonic Orchestra, the Welsh National Opera as well as the Purcell School. The year 2000 saw him restored the tradition of naming Harpists for be a part of the Royal Court by naming a Prince of Wales Official Harpist. While a student at Cambridge the University of Cambridge, he performed as part of the Bach Choir twice and played the cello. He was a part of the Trinity College drama company Dryden Society and was featured in revues and skits. He was also a member of the Dryden Society in 2002. Charles created his own foundation, the Prince's Foundation for Children and the Arts to help kids to be more involved in the arts. He is chairman of the Royal Shakespeare Company and attends shows in Stratford-Upon-Avon as well as fundraisers and the annual general assembly. He is a fan of comedy and fascinated by illusions, and became an associate of The Magic Circle in 1975 after he performed an illusion called the "cups and ball" illusion to be able to pass the audition. In 1978 Charles is also the Patron of The British Film Institute. British Film Institute.

Charles is an accomplished and talented artist in watercolor who has shown and sold his paintings to raise funds for his charitable causes and has published books on the topic. In 1994, to mark his 25th birthday and his inauguration as the Prince of Wales in 1994, the Royal Mail published a set of postage stamps that depicted his work. To commemorate his 50th anniversary the paintings of fifty of his were on display in Hampton Court Palace. In 2001, during the Florence International Biennale of Contemporary Art 20 lithographs of his watercolors that depicted the properties of his country were shown. According to reports, the artist sold lithographs from his watercolors for a sum in the range of PS2 million back in 2016, at the shop located at the estate of his Highgrove House estate. In the year 2018, in celebration of the 70th anniversary of his birthday a show of his work was presented by the National Gallery of Australia. Seventy-nine of his works were displayed on display in London from 2022. He is Honorary Presidency of the Royal Academy of Arts Development Trust.

The Montblanc Cultural Foundation awarded Charles his award in 2011. Montblanc de la Culture Arts Patronage Award to recognize his dedication and commitment towards the arts and especially youngsters. Charles took part in a sketch comedy sketch in the production of the Royal Shakespeare

Co's Shakespeare Live! on April 23rd April, 2016. In celebration of the 400th anniversary William Shakespeare in 1616 at the Royal Shakespeare Theatre. The BBC news channel broadcast the event live on TV. In order to settle a dispute regarding the delivery of Hamlet's famous quote, "To be or not to be is the question." Charles made an unexpected appearance.

Charles asked seven artists in the month of January 2022 to paint photographs of 7 Holocaust survivors. The paintings were used in the BBC Two documentary, Survivors Photographs of the Holocaust and were displayed in the Queen's Art Gallery in Buckingham Palace as well as the Palace of Holyroodhouse.

Publications

Many of Charles's books illustrate his passions. Charles has also provided an introduction or a preface to the works of authors, written and presented as well as was featured in documentaries.

Finance and housing

Clarence House, formerly the residence of Queen Elizabeth The Queen Mother, was made Prince Charles his officially London home in the year 2003 after the completion of a PS4.5 million refurbishment. Before moving into York House, St. James's Palace was his main residence from 2003, he as well as his wife Diana resided in apartments 8 and 9 in Kensington Palace. As a Prince, his primary income source was from that of the Duchy of Cornwall, which has 133,658 acres (about 54,010 ha) of land. This includes residential, agricultural commercial and residential properties, as well as the investment portfolio. Highgrove House in Gloucestershire is part of the Duchy of Cornwall, who purchased the property to be used for Charles as a residence in the year 1980. The Duchy rents it out for a fee of PS336,000 per year. It was revealed that the Public Accounts Committee published its particular 25th report on the Duchy's finances in November 2013 noting that the duchy did very well in 2012-13, growing its overall income and earning an overall increase of PS19.1 million in total.

In 2007 Charles bought a 192-acre estate (150 acres for grazing, parkland as well as forty acres of woods) located in Carmarthenshire. The owner applied for permission to turn the farm into an Welsh home in the name of Charles along with the Duchess of Cornwall as well as let out as vacation apartments in the event that the couple isn't at home. A family from the neighborhood claimed that the proposed changes were in violation of the local restrictions on planning which led to the request being placed in limbo until the conclusion of a study on what the changes proposed will affect the bat population in the area. The summer of 2008 saw Charles as well as Camilla were the only guests to stay at the recently constructed Llwynywermod. They also take occasional trips in Birkhall which is a luxurious mansion located on the Balmoral Castle estate in Scotland which was previously used by the Queen Elizabeth and the Queen Mother.

In 2016 it was revealed that his property received an annual sum of PS100,000 in subsidies for agriculture through the European Union. From 1993 onwards, Charles has voluntarily paid taxes under the Royal Taxation Memorandum of Understanding which was revised in 2013. Her Majesty's Revenue and Customs was requested to look into tax fraud from The Duchy of Cornwall in December 2012. It was also requested to investigate tax evasion by the Duchy of Cornwall is also identified in the leak of German newspaper, Suddeutsche Zeitung's Paradise Papers, a collection of personal electronic records that are linked to offshore investments. The documents reveal that the Duchy was a shareholder in carbon credits trading in Bermuda, a company run by Charles' Cambridge friends. The investment was concealed however there is no evidence to suggest that Charles or his estate evaded UK tax.

Styles, titles and awards

Styles and titles

* November 14 1948 - - February 6 1952 His Royal His Royal Prince Charles from Edinburgh

* February 6, 1952 - September 8 2022 His Royal Highness the Duke of Cornwall

* in Scotland in the month of February 1952 until September 8 2022 His Royal Highness the Duke of Rothesay

* July 26 1998 from September 8 to September 8 2022 His Royal Highness the Prince of Wales

8 September 2022 Present: His Majesty The King

When speaking to the King, it's acceptable to address him first as His Majesty, and then to address him as Sir.

Honors and military appointments

Since 1972, the time Charles was appointed an officer with the Royal Air Force, Charles also has held substantive rank in the forces of a variety of nations. In the years since 1969 Charles was appointed as Colonel as Colonel, Honorary Air Commodore and Air Commodore in Chief and the Royal Honorary Colonel. Royal Colonel and

Honorary Commodore for around 32 of the military units across the Commonwealth as well as those of the Royal Gurkha Rifles, which is the sole foreign-based regiment of the British forces. In 2009 and since, Charles has held the highest rank in all three divisions of the Canadian Armed Forces. In June of 2012 Charles was awarded the most prestigious honorary rank in the three branches of the British Armed Forces "to recognize his assistance in her duties as Commander-in-Chief" through the appointment of him as The Great Admiral of Fleet, Field Marshal as well as Marshal of the Royal Air Force.

He is an officer of seven orders and has been awarded eight awards that come from Commonwealth realms. He also has received twenty distinct awards from foreign states as well as the awarding of nine honourary degrees by universities in Australia, United Kingdom, Australia, and New Zealand.

Prince Charles was crowned King Charles III after the demise of his mother. He then was heir to the armorial of the Great United Kingdom.

Conclusion

Are you sure that Charles reign as King?

Probably, one day. However, it was an extremely long journey. It appears to be an heir with an extremely difficult time.

The parents were away so much in his early years. Extremely unhappy being away from his home at Prep School, at least in the beginning and then even more so at Gordonstoun.

Affection for someone he couldn't at the time , marry. In the end, it was an engagement that soon transformed into a loveless relationship was played out in front of the general public.

With him is the villain.

The death of this ex-wife was blamed and placed directly at royalty, with him is the person most blamed.

However, there hasn't been a bad moment. He has a good relationship with grandfather, his sons, and ultimately , his parents.

Of obviously, Camilla.

It could take a bit but the sun is beginning to shine on his way. He deserves it.

www.ingramcontent.com/pod-product-compliance
Lightning Source LLC
Chambersburg PA
CBHW050405120526
44590CB00015B/1829